# Two Worlds:
## Developing Your Psychic Skills

*"First in the Two Worlds Series"*

*by Nancy Matz*

How excited are you to become psychic — dare to seek yourself out in this book!

# Two Worlds:
## Developing Your Psychic Skills
### *by Nancy Matz*

© 1994
Published 1994. Second Printing 1997. ISBN 0-9647802-8

FIRST EDITION

All rights reserved. No part of this book may be reproduced or transmitted, or translated in any form or by any means, electronic or mechanical, including photocopying, recording, or by any information storage and retrieval system, except for inclusion of brief quotations in a review, without permission in writing from the publisher. This work is based upon life experiences and inter-reaction with clientele. (5,000 to 6,000 people).

EDITOR
MARION DOUGLAS
FAIR OAKS, CALIFORNIA

COVER PAINTING
GREG WHATLEY, ARTIST
GRASS VALLEY, CALIFORNIA

TYPOGRAPHY
KATHIE NUTE, WESTERN TYPE

PRINT COORDINATION
DAVID DART, SACRAMENTO GRAPHICS

PRINTED BY
BOOKCRAFTERS, CHELSEA, MICHIGAN

PUBLISHED BY:
CREATIVE SOLUTIONS
P.O. BOX 1212
POLLOCK PINES, CALIFORNIA 95726 USA

# TABLE OF CONTENTS

*Preface* ..................................................................... *i*
*The Cover* ............................................................... *iii*

**Chapter I**
    With Enthusiasm I Want to Say ........................... 1

**Chapter II**
    My Beginnings ........................................................ 5

**Chapter III**
    My Intuitition Kicks In ........................................... 7

**Chapter IV**
    A Lesson in Judging Others ................................. 27

**Chapter V**
    Mediumship and the Continuity of Life ............... 31

**Chapter VI**
    Intuitive Perception ............................................. 35

**Chapter VII**
    Guides and Guidance ........................................... 39

**Chapter VIII**
    Meditation - A How To Chapter ......................... 43

**Chapter IX**
    Spirit ..................................................................... 47

**Chapter X**
    Angels ................................................................... 53

**Chaper XI**
    How Do I Read ..................................................... 57

**Chapter XII**
A Long Distance Allergy ................................. 69

**Chapter XIII**
A Transfiguration ........................................... 71

**Chapter XIV**
On Becoming a Minister ................................ 77

**Chapter XV**
God ................................................................ 81

**Chapter XVI**
Reincarnation ................................................ 85

**Chapter XVII**
Karma ............................................................ 93

**Chapter XVIII**
Soulmates ...................................................... 97

**Chapter XIX**
Discovering a Purpose in Life ..................... 101

**Chapter XX**
Earth Changes ............................................. 103

**Chapter XXI**
"Lady Luck" ................................................. 105

**Chapter XXII**
Other Life Forms ......................................... 109

**Chapter XXIII**
Conclusion .................................................. 111

**How To Chapter**
Meditation and Basic Psychic Development ......... 113

# PREFACE

The day was September 24, 1972. It was a pleasant fall afternoon, moderate temperature, a little overcast. I had invited my sister to a day of shopping and a visit to a new ice cream parlor named Farrell's in the Crossroads Shopping Center across from the Executive Airport. I joined my sister with my 3 year old daughter and was excited to talk to my sister about my new pregnancy. We arrived about 4:00 PM, and talked and visited while waiting for our order. Shortly after receiving our ice cream, I started to feel apprehensive, and more than mildly upset irrespective of my new pregnancy. My daughter had hardly taken a bite of her ice cream. I wasn't sure what was wrong, but I turned to my sister and said we needed to leave immediately. I felt I needed to go home.

Elsewhere......

The pilot had taxied to the runway. His plane, a restored Korean war jet, a F86 Sabrejet, was gaining power for a take off. He was proud of his plane, one of the few left flying. He had brought the plane to an air show in Sacramento. He knew the runway was short so he throttled the plane to full power. As it accelerated he saw a hydrant ahead, then a fence. He sensed a fear as he attempted to lift. He started to strain at the controls. He knew he was going out of control. The plane was aimed for the street intersection ahead. He felt the stress of something about to happen that would change his life forever.....

Meanwhile......

The feeling was getting stronger to leave. I had started to think something was wrong - was it with my home? If not, what? I was feeling that something terrible was about to happen. We left our ice cream unfinished. As I left, I remember the group of people at the wooden picnic tables, the blond girl at the counter, the tall dark boy next to her....

Within a few minutes, going down Fruitridge Boulevard, I glanced in the rear view mirror and saw a billow of smoke.

In the *Sacramento Bee* the next day the headlines read:

# "Old Jet Plane Kills 22 In Crash Into Crossroads Ice Cream Shop."

# THE COVER - ITS OWN SPECIAL STORY

For the cover of this book I had planned on having two worlds overlapping, signifying the idea that I float between two worlds (or dimensions). That is, until just recently....

Bev had come to me for a reading and later brought a daughter to see me. Bev enjoyed both sessions and then asked if I did past life regressions as that was something she was really interested in. I told her I knew of someone who would give her this regression and do it in my home. I asked both parties about a good day and time for both and the session was set.

The evening set aside for this regression was a busy one for me. I had a couple of phone readings and lots of paperwork to do. So, I allowed them to use the front room while I relegated myself to the back office.

I could hear the meditation music start, and when it stopped about an hour later, I assumed the session had ended. And none too soon, as I was really wanting a fresh cup of coffee!

When I went out to the front room, on the way to the kitchen, I noticed Bev was all smiles. She was telling the regressor how life-like everything had appeared to her. She felt she had seen an important lifetime in which she lived in a very large home, in the later part of the last century. I paused for a few minutes to hear more of her story. She was so excited. I was standing next to a wall and a tall white-wicker book shelf in an area dividing the front room and dining room. I began to feel that a spirit was walking towards me. I looked to my right. I could see a hall, an adjoining wall and the tall white-wicker book shelf, and a small, older woman spirit walking towards me! She looked directly at me, giving me a full view of herself from the top of her head to the bottom of her long skirt. I was just amazed! Rarely, do I see spirit so clearly. She was all but in color for me, with shadowing, a good outline of her body and clothing. As she walked to me she put out her left hand and with her fingers bowed just a little she motioned to me with a slight wave of her hand, to reach out to her. Both the regressor and Bev became quiet and were watching me go through some unusual motions. The old woman laid the ends of her three middle fingers of her left hand in the palm of my right hand as I reached for her. Then she pointed to Bev, with her right hand, as if to say, "I'm for her."

I gave Bev a full description of the woman, from her facial features to her clothes.

Bev turned to the regressor and said, "That's the same description I just gave you about the mother I had in that lifetime!" Evidently, spirit also knew of the plans for the evening and felt it would be a good time to reinforce for me and for Bev also — that the continuity of life exists.

Sometimes we receive the proof of our doubts, even when we are not asking.

A few months ago, I was thinking of my book cover again, trying to figure the size, color, etc. I was in my kitchen and I started to get strong feelings that I should call Bev. I have seen so many clients that to arbitrarily think of one particular client so strongly, confused me just a little. Towards the latter part of that day, the same older spirit woman presented herself to me in my house. She greeted me with a smile, and with the same hand gesture. I knew I would have to put her on the cover of my book. As I thought about that - she disappeared! It was as if to say, "OK I did what I was supposed to."

The cover is a recreation of our hands as the woman and I greeted each other that first night we met.

Thank you - to Bev's former Mom - from so long ago.

## ACKNOWLEDGMENTS

To those unseens who have gently guided me through my life's lessons to my chosen path. To those in who I have given my trust to guide and give me the precious assistance and patience to see that my development grew with a firm foundation. To the thousands of you who have allowed me to **"Read"** for you and **"Learn"** from you!

Thank you again, with love,
*Nancy Matz*

## Two Worlds

# I

## WITH ENTHUSIASM I WANT TO SAY

I have written this book with the same belief, the same enthusiasm, the same power that I teach my classes and conduct my lectures. If you were here sitting with me, I'd be sitting across from you, looking into your past, seeking information in your present and future to help you with your chosen Path. I'd be moving my hands and arms and getting very excited with the information I'd get especially for you. Many times when relaxing with friends or acquaintances (and of course with their approval) I'd input psychic information or tell of people, who, in spirit, have come to join in our conversation. In groups where spirit wished to talk to loved ones, I am always amazed to see their loved ones step forward anxiously to have conversation with me. I am always amazed that loved ones in spirit will frequently show themselves to me at a younger age. Their family member will be equally amazed at how accurately I would then describe their deceased family member. I always get so excited. I have learned, of course, not to let all these beings step into me, for surely, I would not have the stamina to last for any length of conversation.

Even as I write this I am getting energy surges as though beings around me are saying, "Write about me! Remember Me - I am the silly one from the other night!" This is not ego, but a wanting to let us know that they have survived the "Transition."

What about these spirits, these beings, who exist in another dimension? And what about beings who exist in other realities? Are you struggling with this idea, that we are not the only living beings in the universe? My gosh! When I started seeing these other beings, if other people were with me, I'd stop and stare or flatly say "Wow - can anyone else see them?" Often when the being would ask me to repeat something to a loved one, the being would frequently say something that would have special meaning only for a relative. The information from the being would often be bizarre or even embarrassing. Throughout the following chapters I will tell you of some of the funniest stories and of course, some of the most bizarre!

I can see, hear and feel other dimensional beings. Yes, I am very psychic, but how does that help you "The Reader" of this book? Well first, I like to tell stories of my funny adventures into the world of the psychic and secondly I'm going to give you very basic developmental information on how to become more psychic. I want you to get as excited as I was the first time I saw and felt the presence of another dimensional being! I want you to be able to access your **higher self** or your **guide** or to **see angels!** To access, and to monitor the wonderful psychic world around us is to alleviate the fear of death, to understand that we, as energy beings do survive.

Spirit has told me that we are here to learn, and experience all that we can for spiritual growth. All human experiences, whether you would call these experiences negative or positive, are life lessons. As we experience human life, we should be able to call upon our psychic gifts to help us through all stages of growth. We can ignore available guidance and chose to blunder through life. Many of us have known people who do just that. Aren't they a mess! It would be much more fun, and we would spiritually grow much faster if we learned to trust our psychic abilities. Yes, some people will have to work hard to learn to relax and to develop their particular gifts. I will address this struggle. I will tell even those of you who might believe you have no psychic ability, how to turn these psychic abilities on. I am the first to admit I have a "hard head". I am the kind of person who needs to have someone "prove it to me" so I can believe it. People have called me "A Funny Nut," "Bull Headed," a "Comedian," "Psychic/Medium," and with all that, I feel my greatest talent that I will be remembered for, will be my straightforward approach to teaching. Nothing has given me greater pleasure than to explain how to use the natural psychic gifts that WE AS ENERGY BEINGS ALL POSSESS. With my stubborn attitude I have heard people say, "If Nancy now believes in this, then I can also believe, because she has this belief - without doubt." People have seen me in public settings, becoming absolutely flabbergasted about knowledge that has just been given to me, or arguing with a spirit about their message or attitude.

Spirit has often joined me in quiet time and given me words of wisdom and encouragement. Once, when I was particularly upset with myself over something very mundane, I received some interesting words to help me understand life's meaning. I call them the 3 L P D's.

> You have received the most precious of all gifts - **LIFE.**
>
> Fill it with **LOVE** and **LAUGHTER** for yourself and others.
>
> Through your experiences identify your **PATH**, recognize your **PURPOSE**
>
> and, of course, most of all, enjoy the **PASSION** for living.
>
> Without this understanding you will create **DEATH, DOOM** and **DISASTER!**

## My Special Prayer

I am a "direct" sort of individual. The more "direct" that spirits are when talking to me, the more "direct" their information is received by me. The more "direct" I can be with my clients, the happier I am.

During the first year of my enlightenment, spirit again inspired me, and gave me a wonderful prayer that I use daily. I'd like to share this rather "direct" prayer with you for your own personal use.

> *I am of the highest vibration*
> *And the purest of mind.*
> *I am a Child of the Light*
> *And a Child of God*
> *Nothing can hurt me unless I believe it so.*

As simple as this prayer is - I believe spirit wants us to understand that we are what we believe to be **"our personal truth."**

I will teach you by instruction, illustrations and interesting stories to help you identify and develop **your gifts.** I will teach you to apply this knowledge to your life, to be spiritually, psychically in tune to all the wonders of this gift called the **human experience!** All the stories in this book are taken from taped sessions, both private and public. My friends in the greater Sacramento area in California and from around the United States see if you can find *your story* in the pages to come. I have been careful not to print any last names, as my clients know privacy is very important to me.

# II

## MY BEGINNINGS

After much contemplation and several rewrites, I've decided that some of my past experiences need to be told - but - I want to keep it VERY brief. I know you want to get on to the GOOD stuff about how to become more psychic! However, a quick trip into my past may just help you to understand some of the struggles you might have had in your past. Some of these difficulties and struggles might have been caused by some over sensitivity due to your unrecognized psychic abilities. If we have psychic abilities that are causing us to see or hear or know something that is beyond our five senses, but we are unaware of our psychic abilities, we can be caught off guard and experience difficulties.

I need to reflect back to childhood and think of my father who died when I was six years old. I remember jumping into his arms one day and saying "Please don't go, we'll never see you again!" The next memory is about his mother and step-dad coming to my house a few days later and telling my mom of his death from a car accident. As a teenager with a vague memory of this incident, my fathers' mother, whom I called Bobbie, not only reminded me of this memory but also said that I had told her that my father had come to visit us the next few nights after his death. Bobbie had recorded our conversation on a reel-to-reel tape recorder, and I was able to listen to it over and over again. At the time I listened to this tape, I was not aware of the potential of my gift. Now I fully acknowledge that I have psychic gifts and that I received my wonderful psychic ability from my father and his mother.

A few months ago my mother told me that three days before his death my father asked her, that in the event something were to happen to him, not to mourn - but to allow him to go home. His mother claimed both psychic and healing abilities. My mother also told me that when she was newly married to my dad, my dad and his mom would have "mental communication" while occupying different residences.

I did not fully understand the importance of this psychic gift until 1986. I was in my mid-30's when I told a friend of an impending death. I told her she would be at work around seven in the morning, receive a call and be responsible for some paperwork due to this death. Within ten hours after telling her of this, there was a murder in her immediate family. She found out about the death the next day at work via phone call at 7 in the morning. From that experience I realized I did not have an over active imagination! Something else was going on! I started reflecting back on all the times I quizzed myself on why I'd think this or that about someone I'd walk next to. I thought about the physical discomfort at being around someone who was sick or upset. I'd visually see cars pass me on the freeway and change color, some I'd see banged up and on rare occasions I'd sense death. I'd have trouble shopping in malls or going to the movies without a lot of personal discomfort. Though I then labeled these experiences as psychic intuition, I still did not know how much my life was affected by this ability, this intuition. I did not know how to control this ability, or that I needed to.

Now I can look back and understand why events in my life were so stressful. Taking care of Bobbie my grandmother in her later years, living through my troubled marriage and other family strife caused me immeasurable pain and suffering. My special sensitivity to people around me meant that I was rubbed raw, bombarded, attacked by the emotions and events around me. After the passing of my grandmother in 1986, difficulty in my marriage and family life the next year, I discovered I had cancer. I had several surgeries in late 1987. The following summer, I ended my marriage of 21 years.

## III

## MY INTUITION KICKS IN

### My Birthday, 1990

A friend of mine named Dennis told me of a phrase I'd like to share with you. I'd like you to think of a time that you have wished for something. Not with selfishness, but out of pure thankfulness. When a prayer is listened to, and the time is appropriate, this prayer is called a "high-risk prayer." At the minute you wish for that special something, you suddenly realize the heavy impact of it, the wish, the prayer. You realize this prayer could change your life forever. It is a "high-risk prayer."

Reflecting back to my birthday on Monday, April 30, 1990, the year I turned 42. I now realize that my friends, the **"unseens,"** were waiting for a signal from me. My unseen friends were waiting to help me start on my path of psychic unfoldment and teaching. After all, if the following amazing events hadn't happened, if these unseen friends hadn't nudged me and guided me you wouldn't be reading this story!

On that particular birthday, I had been thinking of the two years that elapsed since my cancer surgery and treatment had ended, it would be two years in July that I had ended my marriage. My time was well occupied. In addition to my full time job, I had joined a skin care company and was promoting their products. I also had acquired some exercise equipment and had a routine which was keeping me in shape. Of course the threat of recurrence of the cancer did concern me, but I felt healthy and above all, I was grateful!

Driving home from work on this birthday, I was thinking about a couple of birthday cards I received offering "congratulations!" These cards really meant a lot to me. I was bouncing back from sickness and I knew my family problems were finally behind me. On the freeway going home from Auburn to Roseville, California I gave a great deal of thought to my life. I felt I finally knew who I was and where I was heading. As I took the Atlantic Street off-ramp into Roseville, and mindful of a heart filled with gratitude, I said out loud the following high-risk prayer:

> ***Thank You for my life and my sanity***
> ***and if You wish***
> ***I will work for You the rest of my Life.***

At that moment I was not directing my prayer to "anyone" in particular. I just felt I needed to voice my thankfulness. With all that had happened to me in the prior three years, I was not sure at the moment I said this prayer if I believed in God anymore, I just felt I needed to say thank you to someone. Seconds after saying this prayer, I was overcome with goose bumps and a sense that my car was full of people who had been listening to me!

For the remainder of the week I didn't experience any profound events or revelations. Friday came and after a hectic work day, I decided to participate in some "Shop 'Til You Drop," action at a local shopping mall. Again, a feeling of needing to leave overcame me after only an hour of shopping. Frustrated and not understanding this seemingly psychic feeling - I headed home. While driving back to my home, I felt a need to take a somewhat different route.

Now I want to say here that many of you reading this book have had experiences that you would call "guided". Others would say "miracles" had greatly affected their lives. The **unseens,** this day, were about to change my life forever!

Following my feelings to take a different route home I

was driving down a street called Auburn Boulevard in Citrus Heights. On my right a sign seemed to capture my attention. It read:

### Spirit of Grace Spiritualist Church

I felt a tug to my right, the steering wheel and my arms were turning! Before I knew it, I found myself in my car in the parking lot in front of the church.

"Hold on a minute," I said to myself, "I don't really want to be here!" I was just starting to back out when a tall and somewhat lanky looking gentleman came out.

I was invited in to meet his wife, to see that this once small older home was now converted to a church. I had serious reservations. The woman was the pastor of the church and welcomed me to come back in about an hour to participate in the Friday night 'circle' and practice "psychometry."

**Psychometry?** I had never heard the word before - what is that word about?

I remember thinking, that I had felt compelled to come into this parking lot and that I might as well come back later to check this out. No harm could certainly be done.

A small group of about eight people came to the church that night. A prayer was said. Personal objects were collected and the co-pastor asked that all be quiet. He picked up a ring off the tray, held it in his hand. He was sitting next to me and I noticed that he seemed to concentrate on this ring with his eyes closed. All of a sudden, he said "I see this woman....." and all sorts of personal information came forth, all based on the ***"vibrations"*** of the ring.

To say that I was surprised was an understatement! Never had I witnessed an activity like this. After I calmed down and relaxed, I looked at his hand. Without knowing how, I too began to receive information in my head about the same woman! I was getting the same information as he was but seconds before he would say it.

Before a second thought could catch my tongue, I asked, "Would you mind if I tried that?"

He looked at me and then he looked quizzically at his wife. He handed me the ring. With that single action - my world changed forever!

The feeling of energy, information, wonder all came at once! I tried it again, with another object and then another! Information flowed out of me...the hunger to learn about the psychic world had just been started.

That was Friday evening, **May 4, 1990.** It was only five days after I had said my prayer, and there I was in this spiritualist church, *"reading"* by psychometry and not a clue on how I was doing it!

Attending some classes, I finally figured out how to control my gift. Through psychometry I learned to **"turn it on,"** and how to **"turn it off."** I learned how to *"focus"* and to keep my readings short and precise.

Reading objects (psychometry), I started realizing that perhaps we as human beings had energy around us that we could leave behind on objects that we wore or touched. I understood that all of us have an *"energy field"* around us. Is this what we left on objects? The church ministers taught me a new term - *"vibration."* Vibrations were energies that people left behind on objects they touched. These energies or vibrations could be read by psychics.

As the weeks passed, I discovered I could read the vibrations of family members and friends, and of those individuals attending the church circle by using a process I call *"bridging."* Through the vibration or energy field of the individual I was reading, I could literally "see," "feel," and "hear" virtually any individual they knew and wanted to ask about.

Shortly after that I then learned I could "see," "feel,"

and "hear" **spirit.** I found much to my surprise I could describe deceased family members and friends of these individuals. From the deceased family member, I could bring *"messages"* that not only made sense, but were appropriate to the personality and experience of the departed loved one. The gift was literally overwhelming to me. At times I was apprehensive, but the experience was so exhilarating!

I want to emphasize here, that before the day I entered the spiritualist church for the first time, May 4, 1990, I'd had psychic experiences, but hadn't realized how to control the gift!

## *My First Reading*

On June 6, 1990, one month and two days after I stepped across the threshold of the Spirit of Grace Church, I gave my first private reading in my home. I suddenly became enmeshed in issues I never gave much thought to in the past. Whenever someone new attempts counseling many of us will want to perform this service for free because we feel it is a gift to be shared freely. I have and continue to give hours of lecture and group talks free (with discretion). As a business, I do private or paid group sessions. I would encourage you also to follow a similar format, your time and gifts have value.

If you pursue this path, there will come a time when you may become overwhelmed. Always remember to value your own personal life as much as you give importance to clients' personal lives! Always keep in perspective that no matter what career path you pursue, there will always be the highs and lows — negative and positive moments. There are always people who will seek you out for the purpose of having you live their lives for them! We cannot assume we have the right to live someone else's life. Spirit has told me that one of the big sins in the universe is to take **"free will"** from someone. Be careful not to make decisions for someone and take their free will. This is a thought I will debate for hours with anyone. If I am able to see years of growth for a young child, or obtain a future view of decades of marriage or business decisions, have I already seen your choices? If so, has your choice already been determined? And if I see the end result of your choice can we then call that choice free will?

Getting back to this first client. Although I was admittedly nervous, the client was very tense and under a great deal of stress. Our session together required as much counseling as it did psychic ability. As I will tell people, being intuitive is good but only as good as your ability to communicate the information in a manner acceptable to the client. I would encourage anyone wishing to counsel others to receive some training on communication. I received good advice from a fellow reader once: "When you are confident of your talent, and a session with a client is not all you wished it to be — always remember that it is the client that sets the **truth** of each session." I have also learned that extreme stress or a client on heavy medication can hinder my reading of the client. I attribute this to the fact that I call myself a **"hot"** vs. a **"cold"** reader. Being "hot" means that I'm very empathic and if the client's energy vibration around their body is too tight or stressful, it can be almost impossible to penetrate. I have friends with some psychic ability, who use tools (tarot, etc.). These friends do not totally step into their client's energy fields. Some of the feedback I get is that their readings are a little less personality detailed.

### *Drawing - A Child Yet To Be Born*

Because I was so anxious to do well, with my first client, I remember feeling very shaken after finishing that reading in my home. I felt completely drained. The pastor of the church and I had been getting together on Tuesday evenings to give me instruction in the technique of *"psychic art."* I gathered some experience in drawing spirit while participating on the church's Psychic Sundays, a time when the church offered mini-readings to the public. I had made an appointment to meet with the pastor on the evening after this first private counseling in my home. When I got to the church the pastor was sitting at a table drawing. I told her about my first reading, about the stress the woman was under, and about my reaction. She smiled and said, "why don't you ask spirit to help you draw something that would make you happy?"

In the next hour, I was to learn something from spirit, on the **"process of selection."**

We had some pastel colors on the table between us. I ran my hands over the various colors and selected the "warm" blue one. Somehow the blue one felt "more important" than the others. With chalk in hand, I began drawing an oval. It didn't feel quite right, so I started over. When I finished, I had drawn a picture of a sleeping infant.

In a perplexing manner I explained, "I've drawn a picture of a baby sleeping!"

Her reply was "You ought to ask who it's for."

The moment she spoke those words I saw a vision of my daughter, Jenny, standing there in front of me. I understood the light-colored mist to be a soul essence swirling all around her. I then heard the words: **"a selection has been made."** I got quite excited, not believing what I had heard.

I described my vision to the pastor, who in turn asked quite logically, "Is Jenny expecting?"

I didn't think so. Jenny already had one child, my granddaughter Jaclyn. As a rational, protective mother, I didn't think Jenny needed any more children. Although she and Mark Elliott were living together at the time (I subsequently married them on May 15, 1993), I was pretty certain that adding another child right away was not on their agenda.

*14 Two Worlds*

I went home and called her. "Jenny, are you expecting?"

"Mom, of course not!" She was emphatic and sounded a bit exasperated with my question.

That was June 6, 1990. Toward the end of August I received a call from my daughter, "Mom, guess what! I'm pregnant!"

I was overwhelmed, not because I was going to be a grandmother for the second time, but because spirit had told me of the conception of a child some two months in advance! I called the pastor of the Spirit of Grace. She and her husband had gone to bed, but I had to tell them.

"Guess what? she's pregnant!" I heard acknowledgment from the other end of the phone call that spirit had wanted me to know something special that past June.

Samuel Harrison Elliott, was born April 10, 1991. When he was four hours old, I took a Polaroid picture of him. The family and I compared the photo of the baby

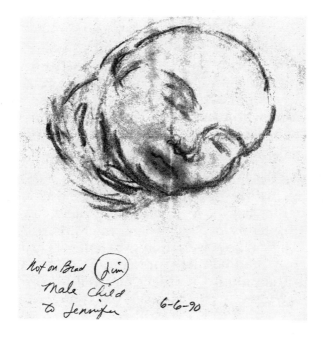

⇒ Two Worlds 15

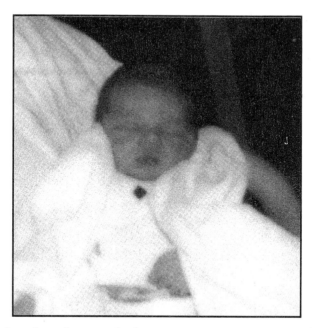

with the drawing and they were an exact match. *(See drawing page 14 and photo above)* Interesting enough, the night I drew the drawing the color of the chalk was "blue," the color often associated with "male" child.

From my numerous readings that I have done and from the conversations I have had with spirit, another truth has become known to me. The essence of the child begins to associate with the mother as much as a year in advance. In the event of termination of a pregnancy, the soul essence of that individual will stay with that mother if a full term pregnancy is to take place in the future. If a full term pregnancy and birth are not possible, the child's first choice **"vehicle parent,"** (mother or father) will still interact with that child at some time in its life.

Here is another interesting story of knowing about a pregnancy before conception.

In September of 1992, I read for a woman whom I shall call Bev, thirty-eight years of age, divorced and the mother of a five-year-old boy. She is employed at a military complex here in Sacramento.

# 16 Two Worlds

During the course of our reading I described a female child with silken brown hair around her, a beautiful child about the age of three. Bev's reaction was "Well, I must be married then because I wouldn't have a child without a husband. What does this man look like?"

In some detail I described a man coming to her — let's call him Bob. I found him to be in the same professional field and that the two of them had similar interests. I was just getting too much information for this to be an overactive imagination on my part.

She met the man just before Christmas. Bev discovered that they did indeed have similar interests and were in the same field. She also learned he was in an unhappy marriage, but the timing just didn't seem quite right to start a relationship. She knew they would meet again.

Two months later, in February, they did meet again and she found not only had he lost weight, but he was far more handsome than she had remembered. It was obvious that he was attracted to her (as she was to him) but he was still married. However, being in the same profession, he stated he was interested in transferring to her military complex.

In the meantime, being a normal woman with normal needs — that is, needs for companionship and the affection of the opposite sex — she had "a small fling" in late May. She soon found herself pregnant by a man who presumably had a successful vasectomy.

In June, she learned that Bob would be transferring into *her* military office in July. Would the possibility of a personal relationship with Bob be ruined because he learns she has become pregnant by another man? Is this child really "Bob's child" who has accessed him as the father, through another man?

Carrying this one step further, if Bev should have the appropriate medical tests for a woman of thirty-eight, or of any age for that matter, and learns that the fetus is female, this fact would fit my gender description. Should this knowledge influence her decision to carry the fetus to term? Or should she have an abortion and give the soul essence another opportunity to try and come through again, this time via Bob? If she was pregnant with a male fetus, perhaps my determination of the sex of the child was wrong. We have all been wrong at times. Even Abigail Van Buren (Dear Abby) and Ann Landers have admitted in their columns to being wrong from time to time, and to the best of my knowledge, they make no claims for having psychic ability!

If you were close friends with Bev, how would you advise her? With her child, we have a soul essence who wishes to reincarnate through Bev. Did the "momentary fling" create the right pathway or should she start over and hope to try again, this time with Bob? Should she gamble and discuss her pregnancy with Bob? Should she bring the information from her psychic into the discussion? At this writing Bev's decision has not been made. What advice would you give?

Every pregnancy offers us wonderful opportunities for growth and greater understanding. Therefore, if a pregnancy occurs, is it for the potential parent's learning - or for the soul essence to learn more about the human condition?

At the time of the printing of this book, we will have found out if Bev keeps the pregnancy and what the sex of the child is. Turn to page 112 of this book, for the outcome!

### *"For Your Mom"*

While I was at the church drawing the picture of my future grandchild Sam, I had the sense of some control over me. I was not randomly trying to draw any particular person or a sleeping infant. Only when I finished the drawing, it occurred to me that this was a drawing of an infant! Another drawing that came through me, also came with instruction to whom it was to be presented! While it seems obvious that a spirit will assist me to draw his or her own picture, the identity of the spirits responsible for assisting me in an informational drawing is usually not known.

 I have always stated that going into this psychic arena, was a surprise to me. I had not told my mother of my involvement in the spiritualist church or that I was practicing psychism or mediumship. I wanted to tell her but was not sure how she would respond. While I was growing up, my mom did not discuss the **"family"** gifts. **"The unseens"** must have realized that my mother was uncomfortable with psychism. So, one night at drawing class, I felt a sudden urge to draw. Allowing my arm free rein, the unseens guided me to draw a girlfriend of my mom's who resides in Marysville. What makes this unusual, is that I drew my mom's friend as a child when they met, not as the woman she is today. The spirits also furnished me with information on her as a child and as an adult. They had me write on the top of the drawing, "This is in confirmation of my belief." After I wrote it I realized it was meant for my mom. When I showed the drawing to her, her comment was "Why that's a picture of my girlfriend, Helen, when she was a girl! But, you haven't met her yet. How did you

know what she looked like?" I cannot take credit for the drawing and I will acknowledge spirit as the "artist."

At a drawing session, I will allow a gentle force to control my drawing arm. The drawing of young Helen was quick and with clean features. I was done in a couple of minutes. I do have an artistic background and have favored portraits with pastels or oil as my medium. What is particularly amazing to me is that my chalk drawings are done easily and with far more skill than I would draw when **not in trance.**

## *Someone With a Sense of Humor*

Someone who has passed, will often keep that part of a particular lifetime's ego that they enjoyed the most. At drawing class one night, one lady who I am particularly fond of named Nancy, sat next to me during the session. I started right off with vigor, I was drawing a gentlemen with his hat so crooked. I said to her, "He says he is from your family, and would like to see his picture on the wall above your dresser."

She agreed. She took the drawing home, framed it and placed it on her dresser, not on the wall as she was instructed. Two weeks later she came back to class. "I went home and placed the drawing on my dresser. Several times the drawing would end up face down on the dresser. I'd set it right and the next time I'd walk by the drawing again it would be face down! Really curious about this persistent man, I went through a trunk up in the attic and found a photograph which matches the drawing exactly. The man you drew is an uncle of mine, long since deceased. I put that photograph and drawing side-by-side, on the wall, where we both could see them."

My artistic ability is noticeably better while in a light trance. I **"*drop down*"** into the light trance that invariably overtakes me when I am drawing or giving a reading. Once I "drop down" my drawings flow quite easily. There was one exception.

I was drawing a picture of a grandmother for a client during a Sunday afternoon psychic fair at the Spirit of Grace Church and I was having a terrible time. It was just awful! When I finally drew the older woman so that she was recognizable, the granddaughter said: "I thought you were drawing my other grandma. No wonder you had trouble. This grandmother was left-handed! Besides, she had a stroke which not only left her paralyzed but the stroke ultimately took her life! Now that she is in spirit, not only was she adjusting to the effects of the stroke, she was trying to manipulate a right-handed person!"

On another occasion a gentleman in spirit came through. He was a man with a strong personality who told me he had met the co-pastor of the church in the 1940's when they were both in the Navy. I found myself drawing feverishly and with power. When finished I showed my drawing to the co-pastor. He said immediately, "Oh, that's Hallet. I knew him in 1944." I relayed the information, I received from spirit Hallet with the best interpretation I could. After Hallet left the Navy he returned to the east coast, had children and died in 1952, or was he 52 when he died? I think he told me he was from the Bronx.

The art of "mediumship" or the allowing of a spirit to be incorporated into living flesh - sounds strange doesn't it?

## Candle Drippings

There are a variety of intuitive techniques through which you can develop your inherent gifts. One evening, June 18, 1990, our study group tried candle drippings. The process is simple enough: relax, ask for guidance and allow a lit candle to drip wax onto a piece of paper. Allow the person next to you to place their hand onto the drippings and to read "your" vibrations in the wax.

The group sitting around a table, each holding his or her own candle, proceeded to create interesting patterns on paper with their wax drippings. I held my candle very still and at an angle in order to get a "nice blob" on a paper which would be read by the person seated next to me. During this process, I experienced the presence of a small child appearing between Lee and Juanita, two of the other women attending the class. As I was describing the child, the child turned and looked directly at Juanita. From my description, Juanita said she recognized the child as being the daughter of a family friend. This daughter had made her transition at the age of seven.

We then exchanged the papers holding the candle drippings and the co-pastor asked Juanita if she could recognize this child if she saw a picture of her.

"Of course," Juanita replied.

My candle dripping paper was passed to her and much to my surprise, spirit had allowed the wax to be molded into the child's likeness. Juanita wrote the child's name, age and year of her passing on the paper holding the wax image to verify what had taken place that evening. This candle dripping is one of my favorite pieces of **"proof,"** not only of an **"afterlife,"** but of the ability of spirit to mold malleable material to a given likeness. This is one example of *"physical mediumship."*

### The Cemetery

The following story was again directed by "spirit." My faith hadn't been as solid as my developing gift. People will talk about miracles and events that are beyond the possibility of random chance. I was about to experience one of those events. Because of this event, my thoughts of *"free will"* and what appears to be *"random chance,"* have been changed forever.

It was now early July. I was reading on a regular basis at our Friday night circles and although the circles were still relatively small, new people began to regularly augment our little group. We had about ten to fifteen people on this particular evening.

One of these newcomers was an attractive woman with very short brown hair, whom I found to be very pleasant. During the course of the evening I looked at her and said, "I do like your hair short. It looks very nice and if you want to buy those flat silver earrings I think they would look very attractive on you."

The woman was momentarily stunned. She told me she had her hair cut that very day and hadn't felt altogether comfortable with its being so short. The short hair was prompting her to consider buying a pair of silver earrings — "big flat ones," she said.

I found this short haired woman, Camille, to be open, soft spoken and very spiritual — but with many serious questions relative to her spirituality. We have since become good friends; very comfortable with one another.

One Friday evening, about a month after the earring episode Camille turned to me and said: "You know, I'd like to take you to a cemetery and see if we can get a picture of a ghost."

I looked at her, mildly amused, and curtly said, "Why? There's no one there!"

"Well, I read in a tabloid that it might be possible to take a picture of someone who was deceased. The tabloid also said you could pick up voices on a tape recorder. I intend to be ready for anything to happen!"

The next afternoon she drove up to my house fully prepared for our cemetery romp. With her came two jackets, two pillows, a tape recorder, a sketch pad, extra paper and two cameras, a 35 mm and a Polaroid. She looked ready for a safari, not simply a jaunt across town to a cemetery. With some misgivings, I gave in, got in her car and we were off to the cemetery.

It was about 4:00 PM that Saturday afternoon when she arrived at my house. It was about 5:30 PM or 6:00 PM by the time we arrived at an area cemetery, north of

Carmichael.

As we drove in, I noticed the cemetery seemed to be in two sections. The right side appeared to be older, with more elaborate markers; while the left side was clearly the larger of the two. I felt we should go to our left and fortunately the gate to the area was still open. With all the "stuff" in tow, I said, "Lead on, Camille, lead on!"

Intrigued with the possibilities of this experiment, Camille suggested we sit in the center of the left-hand section and meditate. My attitude tended toward the practical.

"The caretaker may think we're just a couple of statues, lock up the place for the night, and then we'll be stuck here in the cemetery overnight!"

"You're just a worry wart."

Interestingly, the moment we sat down I relaxed. I immediately sensed the presence of a female near me. "Who are you?" I asked.

"This is Anna."

I saw a female with short hair dressed in a white, flapper style beaded dress.

"I'm Anna. I've been *waiting* for you and if you'll head towards the back side of the entrance of the cemetery you'll find my stone. I'll be near 90 years old." With that the spirit pointed the direction to me. I told Camille the direction we were shown, hardly believing what I had seen or heard. My faithful friend dutifully picked up all of her paraphernalia and trudged along behind me.

"Waiting for me?" I never gave this statement a second thought.

It didn't take us long to find Anna's final resting place. According to the grave marker she was only 87. "O.K.," I said to Anna, "now what?"

"You're here to help someone else," she responded.

"Oh really? I thought this place was empty. Where

should we go next?"

"I want you to find it." With her finger she pointed me in a new direction.

"It?" I kept this thought to myself, not imaging what she was trying to say to me. At this point I clearly thought I had fallen off my rocker.

I relayed all of Anna's information to Camille and she brightly popped up, "O.K., we'll walk up and down between the headstones and see what energy we pick up. You start at one end and I'll start at the other."

It wasn't long before I heard Camille call me over. "These two rows in this section sure give me the goose bumps and the hair on my arms is standing up. This small area here seems to have a lot more energy than anywhere else."

I walked over to her and could feel the energy to which she was referring. We tried to narrow it down, I had slowed down near a gravestone where the vibration was heaviest. Was this the "It?" Anna then indicated to me that she wanted me to look down and see what I could see. As I looked down, I could see a white, shimmering image below ground. "Oh my," I said, "it looks as if some one is sleeping."

"It doesn't happen very often, but this woman has decided to stay with her physical body," Anna explained.

"What do you want me to do about it?" I asked.

"Sit down and pray for her to leave."

I did so, but I could feel she was tenaciously hanging on.

"Try again in about twenty minutes."

My companion was looking at me rather quizzically through all of this.

We waited and then I prayed again. Still the woman appeared to be tenaciously hanging on.

"Later on you'll get something," were the next words I heard from Anna. I didn't know if she meant later that evening or later that year.

"Pray for her for four more cycles," I felt that Anna meant four more Friday night circles at the Spirit of Grace Church.

"All right, Camille, we can go now."

Then I heard the words: "WE cannot believe YOU are so stupid!"

"Pardon me?" I asked somewhat indignantly? I had done everything I was instructed to do, and then I was called stupid? And by someone I wasn't sure was real? And where did this "someone" get this "we" stuff?

I looked at Camille and told her, "Anna thinks I'm stupid because I haven't noticed something." And then I heard our spirit friend say:

"WE have gone to all this trouble to bring you here to prove that WE are real and YOU didn't notice."

"Notice what?"

"Get up and look at the headstone on which you have been sitting."

The woman for whom I was asked to pray for had made her transition on May 4, 1990, the same day I first crossed the threshold of the Spirit of Grace Church to begin the start of a new life and a new me! I'm not sure if the lady in question had been part of the plan to get me there so I'd see "something." What was made very clear to me and to Camille is the fact that because I was so stubborn in my disbelief, Spirit had to convince my friend to read the tabloid, think of that particular cemetery and plot to get me to go there. On the pretense of ghost hunting! This was clearly not a matter of my free will but of spirits will!

# 26 Two Worlds

## IV

### A LESSON IN JUDGING OTHERS

Over the course of my relatively short career as an intuitive and medium, I have had numerous opportunities to read, to provide spiritual counseling and to lecture. Besides the Spirit of Grace Church, my early opportunities included Friday night circles and occasional Sunday morning sermons at the Chapel of the Pines, a spiritualist congregation affiliated with the National Spiritualist Association. In addition, a local metaphysical book store in the Sacramento area provided me with an opportunity to learn a valuable lesson.

This metaphysical book store sponsored a day of readings the first Saturday of each month free of charge to the public. I was happy to contribute my services. I knew there were people in the community that simply could not afford to pay a fee but needed the kind of counseling that my colleagues and I could provide. Beyond that, since I was just starting out, it was good practice and good exposure.

On one of these Saturdays, from among the people who sought me out, one individual in particular stands out. As I stood up to stretch and take a brief respite from my steady stream of clients, I noticed her sitting in the hallway, an immense woman, patiently waiting.

"My gosh," I thought, "I just know she is here to see me." As I sat back down, sure enough, here she came. I thought to myself, "what can I tell this woman, it appears that she has already made her choices. How can I possibly help her?"

"I need some minor surgery," she said as she sat down, "but I need to lose some weight. Will I? Can I? And will they do the surgery?"

Before I could respond I was given the most wonderful vision. I saw a panoramic view of the most lush terrain, a beautiful valley covered with spring flowers; in the background were mountains, covered with snow.

I saw a tribe of ancient peoples. I have no idea who they were and where they were located. I knew they had dark skin, appeared to be nomadic, and lived in the great outdoors. I zeroed in on the woman in the center. I saw a beautiful young body. The feelings I received from the woman in the vision indicated that she was being walked to death.

"How far can we walk? Can we ever stop? I long for a place to settle down. My children die and I bury them on the plains. I have no life of my own."

Such anguish, such terrible anguish. I knew in an instant that this very beautiful woman was the same woman as the individual sitting in front of me.

Suddenly a profound sense of understanding came over me. I realized her role in this lifetime. She was sitting, evolving and spiritually growing into one of the most psychic individuals I have ever met. Quickly the scene changed. I saw this woman weighing much less. Thus I knew the surgery would be successfully done.

Today she lives in Volcano, California and if you find a woman giving psychic classes you will know that she and I have talked and shared. The reason for her weight was to allow her to be less active, giving her more time to focus on her spiritual growth. She wanted to become a teacher and share the wonderful psychic gift she possesses. As she grows those around her will grow as well. I truly admire that woman and respect the process she is undergoing.

The session with this woman taught me not to prejudge. Whether by phone or in person, I now perceive people by their energy field and vibration rate. If I see the client in person, I seem to be blinded by an individual's looks. If I am asked to describe an individual my client has asked about, I seem to back out of the body about a couple of inches or jump out to about three or four feet. It does not matter if this individual is president of a company or a child. I am just excited to feel again, the energy life force of an individual and to communicate with a soul one more time!

30   Two Worlds

# V

## MEDIUMSHIP AND THE CONTINUITY OF LIFE

Mediumship is predicated on the continuity of life; that there is life beyond the death experience and that there are individuals who can serve as intermediaries between both sides of "the veil."

Nothing in human existence is more personal and ultimately of greater concern than the death experience. Coping with this issue has been an integral part of virtually every religious philosophy created and developed by man since he began to think and reason. Integral with this understanding are the two ultimate questions: "Who am I" and "Why am I here?"

Every culture throughout the world has devised a set of "guidelines" to help cope with the fragile nature of our human existence. Virtually all cultures and religions maintain that life is produced by an all encompassing spiritual force and that each of us, a creation of that spiritual force, possesses a spiritual essence — "a soul" — that is independent of matter. Most cultures believe that the personality of the individual continues after the death experience and that communication with the personality of that individual is possible through the intermediate role of certain gifted individuals. In our culture these individuals are known as mediums.

Mediums (prophets, oracles, seers, soothsayers and visionaries) serve two principal roles: 1) They allow us to access departed loved ones, family and friends, thus assuring ourselves not only that they are doing well, but that when our time comes we too will be able to "cross over" to join them and be welcomed by them; and 2) that we may benefit from the broader encompassing view given by those who have advanced into spirit and who are no longer encumbered by the restrictions of physical existence.

Throughout history, whether we view the records of the Old Testament of Moses and Elijah or the New Testament and the apostle Paul's letters to the Christians in Corinth, the gifts of the spirit are underscored. We can look to the "philosopher of Spiritualism," Andrew Jackson Davis, who in 1847 predicted the unfolding of consciousness through spiritual communication.

Here in the United States the use of mediumship and spiritualist circles began appearing shortly after 1848 when two young girls, Kate and Margaret Fox successfully established communication with the spirit of a deceased peddler later proven to be buried in their cellar.

From the "rappings" heard by the Fox Sisters, mediumship expanded to demonstrate a variety of trance manifestations including the hearing of voices, the movement of objects and the manifestation of spirit into partial and fully-realized form. Fraud was so prevalent that interest began to fade and spiritual concerns began to be focused not on the external manifestations of the spirit world, but on the internal essence of who we are. The New Age movement we are now in is the result of this change in focus.

Today mediumship is still in practice, but the greater evidence for the continuity of life comes from those who have had near-death or out-of-body experiences. Our bookstores are being inundated by people publishing stories of their experiences. These stories are exciting to read and hear about, promoting an even greater hunger to learn more about who we are and why we are here.

For others, confirmation has come through hypnotic regression into one or more past lives. Publication of Morey Bernstein's *The Search for Bridey Murphy* in 1956, thrust a Colorado Springs housewife into national prominence. While under hypnosis, she had vivid memories of a previous life in Ireland.

It was Jess Stearn's *The Search for the Girl with the Blue Eyes* that caught my attention from the time of its publication in 1968, the same year that Ruth Montgomery's *Here and Hereafter* appeared. Since then, numerous professional counselors and specialists in the mental health field as well as prominent writers in the metaphysical field have taken a strong interest in the subject. Among other popular books I might mention: Roy Ald's *The Case for an Afterlife* (1968); Ruth Montgomery's *A World Beyond* (1971); Susy Smith's *Life is Forever* (1974) and *Do We Live After Death* (1975); Dr. Raymond Moody's *Life After Life* (1975) and *Reflections on Life after Life* (1977); Dick Sutphen's *You Were Born to be Together* (1976) and *Past Lives, Future Loves* (1978); Dr. Helen Wambach's *Relieving Past Lives* (1978); Dr. Bruce Goldberg's *Past Lives, Future Lives* (1982); Dr. Joel L. Whitton's *Life Between Life* (1986); Michael Talbot's *Your Past Lives* (1987); Dr. Brian Weiss's *Many Lives, Many Masters* (1988) and Dr. Melvin Morse's *Closer to the Light* (1990). The late Manly P. Hall's series of five essays *Death to Rebirth* (1969) is well worth the time of any serious student.

My own gifts as a medium have allowed me the privilege of helping countless individuals concerned with reaching out to their loved ones as well as helping those individuals seeking counsel from those in spirit. In addition to psychic input, the insights of spirit during a session with a client can be very helpful in calming the fears of the death experience; why someone passed when they did, and how a loved one is doing. Also, knowing which spirit is guiding a client and how to reach a spirit guide will often help to explain the "why am I here" question.

In your search to discover your Path and Passion in this life, if it is shown to you to develop your mediumship skills, do so and do so with resounding enthusiasm. I am telling you that no greater pleasure has been given to me than to comfort a grieving family by showing the family glimpses of the survival of life after death. It is in this light that we will deal with the continuity of life issue.

# VI

## *Intuitive Perception*

Eileen Garrett (1893-1970) was one of the most gifted mediums of this or of any century. I have read and re-read her first book, *My Life as a Search for the Meaning of Mediumship* (1939), and identified with her personal quest for an understanding of her extraordinary gift of mediumship.

I have addressed myself in this book both as an "intuitive" (a psychic), as well as a medium. It is both of these gifts that draws clients to me, whether for counseling on any number of issues, or for a better understanding of the course of their lives. This ability is known by many names, "intuitive perception" being one of them. I found what Mrs. Garrett had to say to be very revealing:

### *Intuitive Perception*

"Intuitive perception is that activating principle in the life of both man and animal, which preserves them against the hostile forces of their own environment. This alertness, or hypersensitivity, in all living creatures, is created by the fundamental synthesis of their five senses registering within the physical body; such instinctive vigilance is the foundation of all true self-protection, which means survival. 'Supernormal' sensing is really nothing, therefore, but *a refinement of that dynamic power which propels all life through its own incessant growth and evolution*[1]."

When I began experiencing this gift during that first circle and psychometry session at the Spirit of Grace Church on Friday evening, May 4, 1990, I felt surges of energy going through me. It was excitement and "nerves," to be sure, but it was also something more.

I thought that this "gift" had come upon me all of a sudden, but now reflecting back, I can remember having many feelings and strong urges to do something or perhaps to avoid a particular situation. Before that memorable date in 1990, I thought I had what I believed to be a super imagination, the thought that I could "imagine" what someone looked like or was doing. Now I realize that my gift was "kicking in," demanding to be used. Today I would tell you or my clients when those feelings come to you, don't sluff them off — **pay attention!**

For the first four decades of my life I never gave much thought to being intuitive or whether any people around me might have this talent. That was Nancy, "the outsider." Now that I am much more Nancy, "the insider" I realize that all of us have this ability in varying degrees. I am also in agreement with Eileen Garrett's view that this ability, which she calls "intuitive perception," is indeed "that activating principle in the life of both man and animal."

From primate to early civilization we can see that man began to organize himself into protective groups. He began to depend less on his intuitive instincts and gave power to small group leaders. Man gave power to these leaders to provide the necessary protection, material as well as spiritual if not comfort and warmth. By delegating this power to others, man began to lose his basic instinctive intuitive perception.

Today, as the twentieth century draws to a close and we enter a new millennium, men and women are again seeking to understand the essence of who they are — their spirituality. This search for understanding leads the seeker to the most fundamental of God's gifts — intuitive perception.

Shafica Karagulla, M.D., in her book *Breakthrough to Creativity* underscores this view. She notes that:

> "Today, man is pacing the outer perimeter of his five senses with an increasing awareness of

limitations. Are there things to be sensed which his five senses do not encompass? Is a breakthrough occurring in the field of human perception? Is man breaking through his five sense barriers into the realm of Higher Sense Perception? The human being is a living, evolving instrumentation. It is logical to suppose that a development such as the ability of Higher Sense Perception is a part of the evolutional process[2]."

Stimulated by the diagnostic work of Edgar Cayce — the medical readings Cayce gave over the course of his life — Dr. Karagulla became curious as to how many of her medical colleagues used Higher Sense Perception, particularly in their diagnostic work. She found that many did, although the conservative nature of the medical profession in effect prohibited physicians and other health professionals from readily admitting it.

Anticipating that a question relative to a medical condition may arise in the course of a reading, I always preface each session by unequivocally stating that I am not a doctor and I do not diagnose, but because I do have "x-ray vision" and because I am able to follow an individual's time line, I can often anticipate certain conditions which may suggest medical attention. Let me cite one example.

In December of 1990 I had occasion to visit the Los Angeles area and had dinner with Bob and Cindy, a couple with whom I planned to spend the night. After dinner I asked if they wanted to experience a reading since I was relatively new in this field and they had not seen me do this before.

As I dropped down to read them I felt our energies blend thus allowing me, in effect, to be that person. I knew there was a problem. I felt a pain in *my* left leg but sensed that Bob did not have this pain at the moment. I told him that if something comes up in the next few months and this pain is presented to him do pay attention to it and have it looked at. I indicated where the pain could occur.

A few months later the pain did come up and that reminded both Cindy and Bob, "Remember what Nancy said?" So Bob went to the emergency room of a local hospital where the physician on duty diagnosed a very bad blood clot in his leg. The physician added that if Bob had waited one more day, the situation could have been much more serious. Bob was taken to intensive care and given blood thinners. For this particular problem I received a warning, but I want to state that I **do not** get psychic impressions of all future medical problems. Why have I missed the kidney attacks - or the broken limbs — or the times I learned later (on two occasions) of clients who died within a couple of weeks of seeing me? I feel that all information is ultimately given to me by my client. How open the client is to being read, or if the injury would interfere with the normal course of this person's life is perhaps why information as this is not given. Please do not despair, if you do not receive life threatening information. You can not be personally responsible for everyone who comes to you. I know of only one person who could walk on water.

### References

**1.** Eileen J. Garrett, *My Life as a Search for a Meaning of Mediumship.* New York: Oquaga Press (1939), P. 207.

**2.** Shafica Karagulla, *Breakthrough to Creating, Your Higher Sense Perception,* Marina del Rey, Ca: DeVorss & Co. Inc. (1967), p. 17.

# VII

## GUIDES AND GUIDANCE

In the last chapter we discussed intuitive or higher sense perception. Not only does the awareness and refinement of this ability lead to a better understanding of ourselves through ourselves, but at the same time we enjoy expanded parameters in our overall awareness.

This rise in discernment and sensitivity not only puts us in closer touch with our higher selves, but also brings us a greater awareness of the very significant role our guides or guardian angels can play in our lives.

From my understanding I believe we have three kinds of guides: Life, Love and Assigned or Requested. The last category Assigned or Requested guides, are those who provide practical guidance for us on a daily basis as needed. When requesting special assistance, your guide can come from a level vibrational different from your own. Your vibrational level is based on individual spiritual growth. Before entering into a particular life time, we may make arrangements with future family members. An arrangement could be made so that as we again go back to spirit, we could become a guide to the family member still living in the flesh.

Life Guides are biologically connected to us in some way, whether we have known them or not in this lifetime. Because of their kindred affection, they may also be Love Guides as well.

Love Guides are those individuals who have loved us directly such as family members or close friends or indirectly. Indirectly, the Love Guide makes the connection to a person through some other member of the family that the Love Guide knew in life. Let me give an illustration of this second connection:

A secretary in the San Jose area called for a reading and to ask about her guide. I saw a young, slim, long-waisted individual in a light dress, form fitting, with a flare in the skirt, very much 1940's in style. The spirit said she had lived in the 1940's, and was showing me a large black car of an earlier vintage. I immediately had a vision of a rumble seat. The woman for whom I was doing the reading couldn't understand why she would have this person as a guide since she didn't recognize her. The spirit guide explained she had been very close to my client's mother and loved her very much. After the reading the secretary checked with her mother and learned that her mother and the 1940's style woman, I described, were part of a close-knit group that were involved in an automobile accident back in the 1940s. Her mother's friend was sitting in the rumble seat and was killed. My description of the woman matched the mother's memory of her friend in every detail. The woman, now in spirit, had transferred her affection from the mother to the daughter, thus serving as the daughter's Love Guide. The closeness of Love Guides appears to have something to do with what we might call "chemistry."

One woman came to me asking about her guides and said "I don't feel anyone around me. I feel deserted." When I found her guides I discovered they weren't touching in with her very closely. I sensed that in this period of time a prelife agreement was made that gave her complete control in order to learn an important lesson. There were only two guides; one being a distant family member, the other her Companion Angel paired up to her before her conception.

Can we chose no guidance for any particular lifetime? I have often thought this through. Certainly we have, as mentioned in the prior paragraph, our Companion Angel. But, there are some individuals who chose a physical vehicle and insist "I will do this on my own!" And, with rare intervention, generally speaking, they appear to be a mess. Judge not what appears to be a troubled lifetime -

remember do not prejudge anyone! For the lesson chosen to learn in any particular lifetime, sometimes is known but to spirit alone.

When we are in peril, find ourselves in an uncomfortable or disconcerting situation, or require special assistance with a given task or project, a special guide may be requested — on a conscious or an unconscious level — and assigned. One might think of this type of guide as a "special tutor."

When we return to spirit again, what factors determine our options to be guides? A special request previously made before birth? Initially, it seems to me, we look at the long-term, overall incarnative plan. Within that larger framework we may be compelled to assist others. We may feel we can achieve a more effective level of growth by providing guidance. Done in an unselfish, giving frame of mind, we might earn a vibrational rate increase, and thus progression into high realms which is, of course, the ultimate purpose.

My assigned guide, or "protector guide," to use his phrase, came to me very strongly one evening in the summer of 1990. I had a gifted roommate at the time, a woman who had developed her clairvoyance long before I had. I remember on this one occasion she said "Oh goodness, Nancy, there's a spirit next to the door standing near you and its signaling to me that it wants to walk through you." He introduced himself, as my "protective guide," and went on to tell us that his last incarnation was during the Babylonian era, well before the time of Christ. Historically the term "Babylonia" refers to the first dynasty of Babylon established by Hammurabi, c. 1750 B.C. His dress and manner of presentation were clearly reflective of that period. Although I have no personal recollected memory to support this, he claimed that he had been my brother at one time. As he came to me, I put my hands up and found the energy of this individual to be very dense, as he had kept his ego for such a length of time. He had also lowered his vibration rate so that it was compatible with mine thus allowing me to feel his essence. His essence, as close as I can describe, felt like firm Jello. The exercise actually took my breath away.

I am grateful for the Babylonian's presence. Without his guidance and the others who work with him to assist me, my professional work would undoubtedly cease. I am grateful to my Babylonian's doorkeeper, Aaraamak, who carefully screens those spirits who would make themselves known through my consciousness. Attaining life's goals are difficult enough, and without appropriate supervision, it would be virtually impossible.

To the reader who has yet to reach an awareness of and a consciousness accord with his guide(s) and to the reader who wants to have a fulfilling understanding of his or her goals for a lifetime, my suggestion is to meditate and allow only the highest and best vibrations to enter into your energy; into "your space." Once your relationship with your guide is established you will be richer for the experience, not only in dealing with present concerns, but in receiving guidance for the long-term as well. In the next chapter we will turn to the gentle art of meditation and accessing your guides.

# VIII

## MEDITATION - A HOW TO CHAPTER

Meditation can serve any number of purposes including opening ourselves up to the guidance that is our inherent birthright. It has been said that when we pray, we talk to God; when we meditate, we listen to what God has to say! When we meditate we are listening to the power within us, focusing it, and ultimately benefiting in a very unique way. Meditation is a means of turning one's focus from the chaos and confusion of this world into who you really are. At our core we are the essence of spirit. It is to that spirit, that inner core, that we return when we meditate.

Getting started is often the most difficult. Find that special safe quiet space where you feel the vibrations conducive to achieving meditative psychic awareness. You want to go to this place and be able to ask family members to honor your time away from the mundane bombardment of everyday living. Pick a time when you sense your particular neighborhood has also settled down, say 7:30 at night, when their energies are also quieted. We don't need to be blasted by neighborhood vibrations as neighbors go and come from their jobs, fix meals or hurry around. Keep in mind that this is your time. Ask family to allow you to do this daily. This is often the most difficult. Make a promise that quality time spent with your family will be enhanced because of a higher sense of purpose you'll gain from practiced meditation.

When I first began meditating I found myself listening to the creaks in the walls, the air conditioning and so forth. I could feel the floor under my feet and the chair underneath me. I had a hard time shutting down. Then I began to experiment. I found quiet New Age music to be helpful. Those in Yoga and similar philosophies, find repetitive chanting to serve as an effective catalyzing agent. There are many good tapes on guided meditations or just for relaxation. Experiment with some of these tapes if you'd like. Some people choose to focus on a pleasing color, a blue or a green; others imagine an exterior soft light — that is in front and ahead of them. Others prefer an interior light— that is within the body. They create a process of "folding in" or "focusing in" to reach that light.

When I do a group meditation I ask people to reach out and feel the sense of love around them, the relaxed atmosphere the room provides, and the warmth of those individuals present. When meditating by yourself seek the protection and love of the universe. Visualize a sphere of white light all around you representing the loving God force.

Today I can reach a meditative state in seconds. It is a matter of calming down the rapid electric firing of the mind. It is part of the "dropping down" or self-hypnosis process. I found that for me to read someone with any depth or clarity, I have to focus on that person as the most important individual in the world. This means developing total concentration and eliminating all of the other chatter going on in my mind.

Visualization can provide an excellent pathway to a meditate state. One technique I use is to see myself walking into an empty room that is soft and light, blue/green in color. Blue/green being my favorite colors — yellow or red, contrast, is too stimulating to the nerves. Once in this room I visualize myself setting down in the corner and I feel *nothing*. I reach up and put my hand *through* the wall and feel *nothing*. I do the same with the floor. Essentially I am surrounded by nothingness. This process, by giving me a focus of nothingness, calms me and shuts off the mind chatter. Through this self-training, self-conditioning process I have been able to condition myself so that when I make contact with someone or even *antici-*

*pate* that contact, I instantly shut down and tap directly into them. When you achieve that *feel* of nothingness, that nothingness is the sensation you seek because you will know that you are ready to focus.

Many of you have heard me say that as I drop down and seek that focus point, I then turn on the psychic feeling I want to use. Each psychic switch has a particular flavor. For lack of a better term each psychic switch or level of focus is like 31 flavors of ice cream. As you learn to meditate and focus - identify each psychic level or experience you work with as having a certain sensation or flavor.

In a previous paragraph I emphasized the importance of turning into one's self. Listen, sometimes for the first time, to the beating of your heart, the blood rushing through your neck. Feeling the very core of oneself can be very exciting, learning to love one's chosen earthly vehicle, your body. Understand the wonder of life and fully identify every inch of your being. This is essential to meditation and eventual contact with guides and angels. If you haven't identified and studied yourself, how will you recognize that information coming from outside of yourself? Knowledge of yourself and your body will prevent you from confusing your body's essence and your mind chatter (ego) with channeled spiritual information. Through practiced meditation you will learn to remove your human natural desire (ego) to question the psychic information you get. You will be able to take in information and accept the information without doubt. This is the major prerequisite to being a successful psychic counselor.

46 Two Worlds

# IX

## *Spirit*

How do I see and feel spirit? In earlier chapters I cited a number of examples: the drawing of my grandson, the clairvoyant contact with my doorkeeper, and with my guide. Now let me tell you a story of one of the times I came to realize the true feel and nature of spirit.

A young lady from Texas came to visit me for a reading one evening accompanied by two friends from the Sacramento area. As we were getting underway with the reading I felt something bump into me. What I found interesting is that when I put my arms around it, it remained very still allowing me to feel its essence. The spirit was a deceased friend of one of the ladies. When I called the ladies over, all three could feel his essence as well. Apparently he had slowed his vibration down just enough within the confines of my arms to make contact possible. Not only could my three visitors feel the mass of this particular spirit, they also felt a slight electrical charge when they inserted their arm into the mass. The fact that all three concurred on what they felt and how they felt it, provided strong, credible evidence of the continuity of life. The desire of spirit to remain in contact with us was also strongly in evidence.

In our world, spirit is all around us, occupying the same space we occupy only in a different **dimension.** If I kept my spiritual consciousness attuned all day long I would probably be dodging spirit constantly. By incarnating when I did, I chose to live in this physical dimension for a prescribed length of time. My gift of mediumship allows me to see into a spiritual dimension when appropriate and generally when I so desire. I do, however, receive unexpected surprises on occasion. One needs to be able to turn the gift off once in awhile, if one is to lead a normal life.

Similar situations with spirit, as sited in a prior paragraph concerning the young lady from Texas and her deceased friend, have occurred on numerous occasions. Not only have spirits manifested when I am with clients in private and group readings, but they have also manifested when I have been with friends or even by myself. Whoever I'm with, whatever the situation, I find that spirit will generally come to me when requested. With permission Nancy, the human being, has the ability to "capture" and "feel" the essence of that spirit who willingly approaches me. I should add that often there is a touch of humor to the manner in which spirit makes his or her presentation and I love it. Sometimes my home is absolutely filled with these visiting spirits. No wonder I want a larger home!

Through my clairvoyance I see this essence of a spirit as being about four feet high; three and one-half feet in circumference. The appearance is that of a ribbed cocoon, in a translucent creamy color, moving in a rotating manner and clearly being of a much higher vibration than those of us in the physical plane. Spirit essence appears to function in its own vibrational space which is a different vibrational space from that used by a human body. Moreover each spiritual essence maintains an individual vibration rate which sets him or her apart from other spirits in the same sense that each human being has a slightly different vibrational rate from any other human being. I coined a term to help describe this distinction, I am now using the term a **"fingerprint vibration."** You have a vibration rate

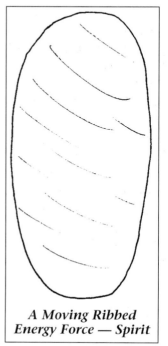

*A Moving Ribbed Energy Force — Spirit*

that is unique only to you. When spirit senses that I have noticed its essence, it will often show me the physical appearance that would be recognized by my client. If I am not in a session, the spirit will appear in the form of their favorite past "ego." And of course when the human spirit vibration rate is compared with that of a different species — a different animal, bird or piece of furniture, the contrast is far more pronounced.

I believe this spiritual core is our **"identifying trademark,"** the essence of who we really are. That rate corresponds to the vibrational level of your particular level of spiritual growth. The companion angel who is paired with you before conception is connected to you and it feels as though the vibration rates are almost identical. Perhaps this similar vibration rate is a way to select a guardian angel with similar spiritual growth and have parity with you. I'm not sure if the angel vibration rate and yours are identical. I feel they are connected to you by an energy cord from you to them, keeping in constant touch with us throughout our earthly experience. When a client asks about their guardian angel, I see an energy force going from them backwards and upwards.

I have had clients who are in love with individuals who have almost identical vibrational spiritual cores. Is this what is generally termed **"soul mates,"** those whose lives are so similar even to the soul level? Those relationships and life patterns, and energy vibrations are almost identical. The concept of "soul mate" does not preclude people who are in loving relationships, whose life patterns or rates of vibrations are very different, from having a wonderful life together. Their contrasting life is what they find interesting about each other, and the lessons presented to each other are also very different.

When a client requests past life information, it is my touching into this same vibrational core that provides me with the information I need. A hypnotic past life regression essentially accomplishes the same thing. The difference between the two processes is that I am able to touch into the requested information instantly, whereas the individual involved in a regression directly "experiences" that lifetime and must sort through lifetimes of information to obtain an answer. One technique can be used to confirm the other.

When a spiritual essence (soul) incarnates into a physical body, the spiritual essence as I feel it, is deep within the center, or core, in each of us. The electrical essence of who we are surrounding us in this lifetime is often referred to as the **"astral body** or **etheric envelope."** Some clairvoyants see this envelope as the aura. I relate this to be the energy created by the pulsing of each atom within our living bodies. Each atom that pulses in our bodies has its own magnetic field. The aura is that energy field created by each electrically charged cell within our bodies. This charge extends beyond the body into the etheric area, into an energy field that surrounds us. Kirlian photography clearly demonstrates this. Further evidence is demonstrated by those individuals who have experienced amputation of a limb. The energy field is still visible and present where the limb used to be. As though the body has memory of a lost limb, the body will create the energy field around the missing limb.

I have seen the aura consist of transparent changing colors. I have seen darkened (or denser) areas of the aura where, like a darkened cloud full of moisture, energy is pulled from other areas of the body to a particular body area for healing. These darkened areas look like funnels, or darkened clouds, or like a ring circling a body area. This aura or energy field around each of us is what I attribute to be a reading tool, that we can use with our psychic ability. I believe that it is not the soul level that reaches out to the client for information but it is this energy field. Those of us with a more sensitive nervous system can move this energy field at will. We can move this energy field to reach out to someone and then back again with collected information. This energy field seems to collect within it, all those ideas, and thoughts most currently surrounding an individual. To "read" information in future time frames or the distant past, I need to merge with the deeper soul level and enter the individual's time line.

It is my view that ultimately we are mental beings of pure thought and pure energy. However, I believe that the personality developed in the last lifetime is retained for an indefinite period, gradually receding once the entity "adjusts" to spirit. In addition I was once told "ego is retained until those living no longer hold memory of that individual." This personality retention means that after an extended period of time your family memory of a deceased great great grandparent is forgotten. Once forgotten that grandparent will not need to pursue the personality of that particular lifetime. When I pass, I am going to look up Cleopatra. With an ego (personality) such as hers, I suspect she is still in that personality. After all, we still talk, and think of that important personality in history, even though it was eons of years ago when she was in the flesh.

When the opportunity arises for a given spirit to present him or herself to me and my client, he or she generally assumes a form based on that earth place incarnation by which he or she can be recognized or wishes to be recognized. Thus a grandparent figure, for example, may present him or herself as they were remembered, or they may choose an earlier age before the grandchild was born because that is the image they prefer and choose to present. Occasionally my client has forgotten that individual or my client needs to talk with others in family to confirm a physical description. What is particularly fun is when I get a call from the client a few days later or receive confirmation at a later appointment. The client overwhelms me with their new found excitement about believing in the continuity of life.

At the time of physical death, the individual returns to the vibrational rate of spirit, of pure thought and pure energy. Yet the individual retains the ego or personality which is the outward manifestation of ego or the "identifying trademark." As the ego recedes, the individual can then choose to go onto further learning or once again enter what I call the "forget sleep" in preparation for reentering the earth plan.

I believe there is a somewhat flexible Divine Plan that governs one's sequence of lives and the learning experiences derived therefrom. What we might call "guided" free will appears to be a major factor in any ultimate decisions, not only within a given lifetime, but in determining the nature of the next lifetime. Time and place of reentry is extraordinarily complicated, since who our parents will be, our friends and associates, our children and descendants all play into the equation. Moreover, we may very well delay reentry. Apparently we have that right if we are unwilling to release our ego from the most recent lifetime. Our reentry into another life may also be delayed because we are held back by the thoughts of surviving friends and family. Clinging to the memory of John F. and Robert Kennedy may be an example of this. Reentry may also be affected by the earthly deeds of the individual in question. It is my belief that Hitler, for example, may find his reentry restricted perhaps for many centuries. I believe he is in a very deep comatose state due to the tragic legacy which he left behind. Thus not only are his deeds (his karma) restricting his progression but we, and generations after us, will not allow him to progress because of our remembrances of his deeds.

The study and understanding of spirit and the nature of spirit is well worth a lifetime of study. After all, what we are learning about is ourselves.

# X

## ANGELS

In the last chapter I discussed spirits and the nature of the spirit world. In this chapter I would like to consider angels and our perception of them. Are they, as more than one philosopher has suggested, "minds without bodies," or are they individualized spiritual beings with form and substance operating on a higher vibrational level that is beyond our immediate perception?

We also need to consider our relationship to these spiritual beings. Are we human beings seeking a spiritual experience, or are we more closely allied to angelic forms than perhaps we realize? Are we really spiritual beings having a human or material experience?

If we are essentially spiritual beings, and I truly believe we are, the basic lesson of the human experience must be for us to develop an understanding of our inherent spiritual nature. We are all trying to grow vibrationally upward to the highest levels attainable to be more closely attuned to the God Force. Have these "spirits" earned the title of "angel", because they reached the highest level of development? Or were the angels always "the messengers of God" or are they "ministering spirits sent forth to serve" as per the Bible in Hebrews 1:14.

We need angels! Whatever our perception of God or the "God Force," because of the fragile, transitory nature of our existence on this earth, we need intervening intelligences — guardian forces — to help us cope with and guide us through the seeming inequities of life.

Religions of the ancient and present-day world say we were created in God's image. Have we created these intervening intelligences as mythological, superhuman figures created in man's image? Or is our concept of angels in human form, often with the addition of wings, a way angels have presented themselves to us so we may accept them visually? They have told me that we would not understand or accept their true nature. I personally have never viewed these beings with wings. I have seen them clothed in man and woman form, as would be socially acceptable to me. I also feel that whatever era an individual has been born into would also dictate how we would perceive them in the afterlife. Earlier mystics who could see the afterlife and/or angels, would see them dressed and socially distinguishable to the mystics particular social attitudes.

After almost five thousand readings that I have done, I find it amazing that I have only had a few occasions where the soul level of a client was shown to me to be of an "angel" level of development. That is not to say, many more of you may also be high vibrational beings called "angels," but these few clients felt it important to tell the physical side of them. Two of these sessions are particularly unique. The first session was a phone reading for a registered nurse in the town of Jackson, California. As I started the session, I "stepped" into her vibration. It almost took my breath away, and in that instant I could see the form of an angel superimposed over the client's body. I was occupied with this vision the entire session. After the session was over, but with the tape recorder still going, I had to ask her - had she ever pursued the study of angels or felt that she had some association with them? I was hesitant to blurt out what I had been looking at for an entire half hour. She stated that her entire life she had felt that she was out of place. As a child she often thought of herself as an angel. She never stated this to anyone. When I told her that I felt that she had come to this life plane to experience the human condition, she almost cried. She had never confided these feelings to anyone before!

The second story is one that took place during a group reading at the Spirit of Grace Church in Citrus Heights. A woman and her adult daughter had come together to the group session. These women live in the Rancho Cordova area near Citrus Heights. The mother's soul level quickly told me that it had experienced only one other lifetime. This lifetime had been exceptionally hard in order to learn as much as possible because the soul had not entered into flesh since the beginning and would not do so again for eons. The soul was of a high angel level. Needless to say, I am usually good with words, but with thirty some people listening I had a hard time conveying this to her. In private, I told her more details. She also told me she had feelings similar to the previous "angelic" client. Having heard what her soul had told me, she became reconciled to the hardships she had experienced in this lifetime. With her remaining years she decided she would approach them with a peaceful attitude.

Like the higher angel levels, I should also add that our departed loved ones and friends are also concerned with their own spiritual development, and also attend and minister to the needs of those still on the earth plane. Their presence is invariably felt in the course of a private or group reading or counseling session. Just as these departed relatives and friends provide guidance and growth to us, there is an angelic hierarchy which provides guidance and growth to them — and ultimately to us. In reality there is no "them" and "us" for whatever level of spiritual development, we are all a part of the spiritual family of God with a mission to help each other.

# XI

## HOW DO I READ

I read and provide spiritual counseling for about a thousand people a year. I also call myself "inter-dimensionally sighted." Clients are always asking how I can see people, past/future events or spirits. Is my vision inside or outside of my physical body? In this and the next few chapters I hope to answer these questions more fully.

To get a clearer idea of how I typically relay information during a session I have selected the following interchange from hundreds of copied readings on tape. I gave this reading to one individual during a evening group session. This taped session was conducted in May of 1993 in Corvallis, Oregon. My friend, Nina, was good enough to offer her home for the evening. To protect the privacy of the woman for whom the reading was given, I am taking the liberty of changing her name. Let's call her "Jaclyn." The reader should note that I had never met Jaclyn and knew absolutely nothing of her personal or professional circumstances.

*Me:* "I know you're new to the group, "Jaclyn," but allow me to read you first. Your energy is real soft around you and it comes way out into the room. I see a male boss around you and he is causing you a great deal of emotional stress. He just has to look at you and I see you shrinking up. It takes a lot out of you and I don't feel good with this. Do you have a question?"

*Jaclyn:* "Yes, is there something from the past that we need to work out?"

*Me:* "He has very sharp energy around him — I feel him during the work day — I started feeling it right away even before we started talking. I feel bodily harm from him in a past life and I'm not sure but he may have been part of a group of people. I would like to look at another blond lady in the office, light like yourself; a little fuller bodied. Who is she?"

*Jaclyn:* "Debbie."

*Me:* "She is also afraid of him. I see her withdrawing. We may have a group of people around him. Who is the younger, dark-haired woman down the hall?"

*Jaclyn:* "Linda."

*Me:* "Her too. So we've got a whole group of you that have known him in the past. I find this situation fleeting, not forever. There is something you may learn from him. Nothing wrong with this man, he just thinks he's better than everyone else and he brings this in from a past life. He's quite emotional himself and has very low self-esteem with the result that he has to be on top of everybody. Very controlling, and that's who he is. He has a real hard lesson and in another two or three years he's going to have a personal crisis that's going to bring him down, so all you have to do is wait it out."

*Jaclyn:* "Am I truly needed in that position. Should I stay?"

*Me:* "For the time being, but you're going past it; you grew past it about a week ago. So you will be looking for something else. I sense you will not be around him when this personal crisis hits. Keep track of this and you'll know exactly what I'm talking about."

In analyzing this brief reading, several points need to be kept in mind. 1) A good many of the people in the group were clients who had been with me for some time primarily by telephone. To create a comfortable working environment for everyone, I usually read "old timers" first. On this particular evening, "Jaclyn's" concern about her work situation was so strong and even though she was a "newcomer," I felt strongly compelled to move into her auric etheric space and read her first. 2) Having intuitively recognized that her work situation was her primary concern, I went through her **"time line"** to the preceding day, and through space to her place of work. This aspect of me which transcends time and space is part of my seeing consciousness or my ***"etheric double."*** It is this double which allows me to be in two places at once. 3) The third step involves a process I call ***"bridging,"*** wherein *through* Jaclyn, I was able to "see" and "feel" her boss and the other members of the office staff. It would have been much more difficult for me had Jaclyn not served as the intermediary or "bridge". 4) By following Jaclyn's time line, I was able to determine that the week prior she had gone past that point where she was "needed." By going forward in her time line I saw that she would no longer be around when the "crisis" hit. 5) By following her boss's time line I was able to assess the *probability* of his future in relation to his personal as well as his professional life, I thus determined that his time remaining in his job was limited.

Examining this reading further, two factors were involved in assessing Jaclyn's situation. Her feelings were clearly reflected in her auric or magnetic field. Which I could easily read. There may also have been some limited telepathy involved. Telepathy involves my reading the thoughts in her mind directly.

Traveling through time to the preceding day and through space to Jaclyn's place of work, not only indicates the relativity of time and space but supports a dimensional perspective vastly different from that which we experience in our everyday physical lives. I perceive an individual's time line as… *(see drawing on next page).*

### The Individual Time Line

That drawing represents an interpretation of an individual's time line. On the time line cord are "indicators." I prefer to call them, ***"markers."*** These markers appear to precede those events we call "destiny," such as career choices, job decisions, partners, life lessons, health issues, etc.

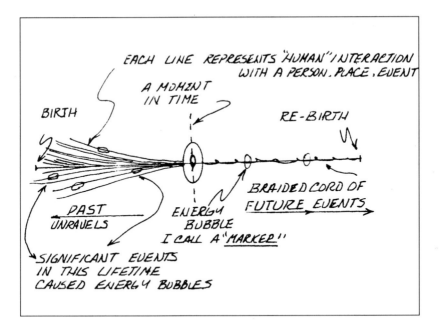

To me, the future is tight like a braided cord. As we pass over each moment, the future loosens and becomes easily accessible. When I am asked about a potential future event, I seem to follow only that "thread" of interest within the "braided cord." The thread makes contact with the marker affecting that particular future decision.

Reading a person's time line is somewhat analogous to the individual frames on a 16 mm or a 35 mm film, each frame capturing a moment in time and space. When the film is run at normal speed, there is the illusion of movement. I follow a person's time line in much the same way. I can go backwards (it feels like slipping - fast, easy) or forwards (like traveling through Jello - thicker feeling), each frame revealing to me a particular life moment. To go backwards reveals a lifetime "frozen" in time and space; to go forward is predicated on the domino effect. That is, what happens in the future is based on what happens now. The future is revealed to me through an anticipated sequence of events.

The time line is a concept I use to help explain the thread which is the progression of our soul from birth to rebirth. When I am asked about future events, once I know the area of interest, the domino effect sets up and I, in turn, follow that thread of interest until I come to "a marker."

A marker can either be an individual or event which precedes *all* destinies. Whatever is important to us in the future is invariably triggered by a given individual or event. This trigger creates the scenario for the event to happen. Thus in following an individual's time line into the future I look for those markers to give me the indicators of what the client may anticipate. If someone asks about a future mate, for example, I look for those markers which will lead me to the events which will bring a new love interest into the picture. Marriage does not come out of nowhere. First there must be the event which brings the couple together, then comes the decision to join together. Someone has to do the asking! Then there is the marriage. The same process can apply to seeking a new job or any other event that has significance in an individual's life. Although markers do, in effect, reveal a person's destiny, our God given free will allows us to make our own choices within given parameters. Should we choose *not* to follow our "destiny," then new parameters are established as a new domino effect is instantaneously set up.

We all serve as markers for others. A "chance" meeting with someone may well change your life as well as theirs. I serve, in effect, as a "professional marker," as opposed to a karmic or a destiny marker, because people seek my advice. They seek my advice on future markers, on how to determine who or what those markers are, and thus, in effect, the clients have greater decision making power, and greater control over their own destinies.

For me to read as I do I have learned to manipulate my energy to extend beyond me to merge with the energy of others that I intend to read. I do feel that this ability has something to do with a very sensitive nervous system. I feel, react and sense emotions at a higher degree than most people. No, I didn't say I was harder to get along with - I just *feel* to a higher degree than others. So when I go beyond myself and merge with others - I can *feel* them easily. I can push my energy as far as I need to and in whatever manner I deem appropriate. Clients and those in my audiences often say: "I can feel the energy coming from this woman and it's enveloping me or coming into my body like an electrical charge. It's wonderful!"

This process begins with a kind of "instant meditation." I "drop down" almost instantly into a mild trance-like state. The degree of this trance varies with the situation. When I am touching into people in a large audience setting, I drop down only slightly so that the flow of the lecture material will not be impeded. When I am reading in a small group setting, I can afford to drop down a good bit further since there is a communal sense to the setting. If it is a private, one-on-one reading I intuitively drop down even further. I find the accuracy of the information is consistent at all three levels. The difference between the levels is that the further I drop down, the greater the depth — *not* accuracy — of the information that comes through. The greater the depth, the easier it is to access past life information, angel or spirit levels, etc.

As to the matter of bridging, I have neither the right nor the reason to intrude into the auric space of anyone without permission to do so, be it the President of IBM or the President of the United States. It is largely a matter of a respect for privacy. However, when one individual comes to me for a reading and the life of another individual in some way directly affects the first individual, then it is perfectly appropriate for me to bridge to the other person to obtain information. I do this through a psychic "encircling" process. *See drawing on next page.* The encircling process allows me to "bridge" from the client to the

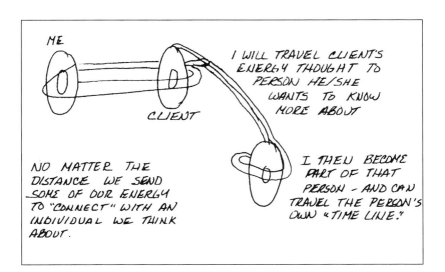

person with whom he or she wishes to make contact, but only in those matters which are relevant to the client. In other words, I can tell if the individual we are locating is "seeing someone" or not, how their business and/or career are going, and even give a long distance health vibration evaluation. What I cannot do and will not do is read the current balance in their checking account! To do bridging or encircling all I need is a first name, sometimes a location and work activity. This information helps me make a sharper connection. When the client thinks of an individuals location and/or work activity the client gives me more energy to follow to find that individual.

I had one of my first experiences at bridging and encircling during an evening circle at the Spirit of Grace in Citrus Heights. A woman asked me to read "Hal" in Reno. I think she was checking up on him! In a split second, I was there and in a split second I was back again.

"He's not there, I can't find him."

"Try Truckee." (California, thirty miles to the west of Reno)

He was there, all right, and doing just fine.

I could never have found Hal on my own, since I did

not know him and knew nothing about him. I needed this woman, his friend, to serve as the bridge. It seems that we create an energy bridge to an individual no matter where they are. At one time I thought we always stayed connected to each individual we have ever met. I now believe that we can create an energy bridge to anyone we have ever met. This includes people in our earliest childhood so long ago that we do not have conscious memory of that individual.

It wasn't long before I began to give telephone readings. On one occasion I was reading a woman in Nome, Alaska, and she expressed concern over her mother in Chicago. I found I could be in both cities and at my home in Sacramento simultaneously. Apparently an etheric double, transcends time and space and can be in several places, simultaneously.

One of my earlier readings also surprised me with a vision. I was talking to a man (John) in New Hampshire. He wanted me to talk about his sister in a coal mining town in New Jersey. Within three seconds I was visually above her house and graphically described her house and surrounding landscape. As soon as my client John said I was right, I was pulled into his sister's body! I was so surprised that I could see with such clarity since east coast time was about 10:00 P.M. at night! It seems that our etheric double can see even in the dark! I cannot remember looking at myself when I'm astro-traveling from place to place. With the focus power it takes to create the etheric double and "travel," to turn around and "look" at my body is something I would like to accomplish - if for nothing else but curiosity.

Although my linguistic ability is limited to English, I soon learned there are no language barriers when picking up information from around the world. One of my most interesting experiences occurred in the fall of 1992 when I was invited to lecture and read aboard a beautiful cruise ship, the *Crystal Harmony.* The operating company,

Crystal Cruises, employs a multinational crew. I believe twenty-two countries were represented — and I came close to reading crew and staff from virtually all of those countries. Italians, Germans, Swedes, Norwegians, Austrians, Filipinos, English and Canadians —and even a healthy sprinkling of Americans were represented. Whether in the St. Lawrence Seaway or out in mid-Atlantic, through the individual requesting my services, I could go back to the home country and answer their questions as to events, friends and relatives. Never hesitate, because of a language barrier, as long as you're able to have someone translate the questions. You'll get the answers in your particular language.

Preparatory to coming for a reading, I encourage my clients to prepare their questions in advance and to write them down! Even though I may anticipate most, if not all of the questions, having a written list does provide focus to the reading and further insures that the client will not leave having overlooked one or two critical issues.

One young woman, Kimber, came to me with a list of fifty-two typed questions. I love her dearly and she is so filled with wisdom for her young age. Her eyes open so wide when we're together and she will say, "teach me everything!" A significant fact is that there is a great responsibility associated with being an intuitive and a spiritual counselor. I take this responsibility very seriously and the reward is in knowing that I, and those who work through me, have helped so many others. I cannot always take credit for readings for sometimes it is so obvious that spirit wants to assist that I have had to put ego aside and say to spirit "go ahead."

Once a young blond woman came for a reading. She had a paper work job in a construction yard office. She said that she wanted to change jobs. She asked if I could tell where her talents were to help give her direction. In almost an instant, a female spirit stepped in and said "Tell her to go back to dental hygiene work!" I was so stunned.

I just repeated what I had heard. The young woman said, " Oh that's just mom, she never did like my leaving that good paying job!" Well, Mom never stopped talking the entire session. Mother and daughter were actually in conflict a few times. I just stopped everything and told Mom - "Hold on - this is my session with her - she wants me to do the reading not you!" The young woman then said, "she always wanted to control my life and she is doing it even in spirit four years after her death!"

I am not infallible. In reading a client's future time line I can see probabilities and about 90-95% of the time I am "right on." I have only received a few calls telling me I was wrong. In one case I told a woman I saw her in a particular kind of job setting. She called a few weeks later to say that no job offer had come through. I asked her what she had done to make things happen and she replied, "Oh nothing. You said I would have such-and-such a job and so I have just sat here waiting for the phone to ring." To succeed in this life one must seek one's opportunities. One must hustle. Now I tell my clients that for my prediction to succeed, they have to go after it. Rarely do given opportunities fall into people's laps. And when they do fall, it is usually to people who have done their preparation and are ready for God's blessing, a new job, or a new opportunity to unfold. Ultimately we are each individually responsible for how we conduct our own lives.

I also remind my clients that I am not a fortune teller. I can read most clients in every way possible, past, present and future. But remember the future is a domino effect from the steps we take today. Do we have the right to know what the future holds? I believe that if the information is given to me, I become a marker for this client. The client has every right to know what I can see and to accept or to change the outcome. If, on the other hand, the future on a given issue is not given to me, it's because the client must make his or her own decision. I cannot and will not take away the individual's free will.

Here is an example. One client had two job offers and wanted me to tell him which one to take. I examined each one and told him the kind of boss he would have. I told him about his working conditions and something about his fellow employees. In other words I gave him a host of details about each position, but I would not make his decision for him. I believe we come into this life with a predetermined blue print. If the blue print is to be changed or altered in some way, that is the individual's right — not the psychics! I will not interfere with anyone's exercise of their free will. What I will do is to give the ammunition he or she will need to make an intelligent choice. I always encourage empowerment of one's ability to make one's own decisions. If I take away this choice, it means that "I" want to live their life for them.

What works for the employee can also work for the employer. One boss came to me and asked me to go through each of his fifty salespeople and give him some insights into the kind of job they were doing, their attitude about their work, etc. I did so. Here is one of my suggestions. I told the boss that there are two people, both of whom I identified by description, stuck off in a corner who are not working up to their maximum potential. I suggested that they should be moved out to the middle of the floor where they can see and be seen. I emphasized that "you will see their attitude and their productivity measurably improve." He followed my suggestion and I was proven correct in my assessment.

To me, my clients become my extended family. I have become very close to many of them. Sometimes they think I have all the answers, and in reality, I don't. I am as hungry for information as they are and I am just as anxious to learn and to grow. When we reenter the spirit side of life our learning continues. Why not accomplish all we can while we are still here on the earth plane.

# XII

## A LONG DISTANCE ALLERGY

In the course of my work as an intuitive, I have developed an interesting clientele in "pockets" throughout the country. One of these is Corvallis, Oregon, the home of Oregon State University. I spoke of a trip in the Spring of 1993 in a previous chapter and the previous year, I journeyed up to this same area in the middle of winter. I had given months and months of telephone readings, and decided I owed my many clients in Oregon a personal visit. One evening was devoted to a group reading at the home of my friend, Nina. The group session had just gotten underway when one of my clients, Stephanie, offered the following funny story:

"While Nina is worrying about the coffee, I want to tell a little story about a reading Nancy once gave me by phone. Nancy is allergic to cats, as I was soon to learn. I was sitting in my kitchen during the reading and I noticed that Nancy was starting to sneeze and sniff and I said 'Nancy, what's the matter?' Nancy couldn't figure it out either. Finally it dawned on me. 'You're allergic to cats, aren't you?' Nancy replied, 'Yes, yes, put it out!' I did as she asked and when I opened the door, Nancy's immediate reaction was 'It's cold.'"

I continued with Stephanie's story and explained:

I felt the cool air come in and hit her because I had already entered the vibration of Stephanie's body. At any rate, once the cat was outside, my allergic reaction diminished almost immediately. I then went on to explain the reading process of going in to and joining with someone.

Occasionally, but thank goodness not often, I can pick up someone's pain or illness symptoms. Sometimes when a client asks that I bridge to someone else and read them, I can often feel their overall health condition. If they have been sick, I might feel weak or tired. If the condition is more serious, I may not get what the disease or problem is, but I'll pick up a very heavy and erratic vibrational rate. In situations like this meditation is very important. You, as a reader, need to know yourself. Do not accept or keep that which you find in someone else. During the course of a reading, if you feel uneasy or are in pain, you need to immediately relax, meditate and release that which is not you before going to another client!

# XIII

## A Transfiguration

A couple of years ago a very popular movie came out called *Ghost*. In the movie Oda Mae Brown, the medium, had opened a psychic parlor, in which she pretended to have dear departed spirits of family members come though her - "for a fee." The first few times that a "real spirit" came through, Oda Mae, played by Whoopi Goldberg, was overwhelmed and she seemed to "puff" out. I would not encourage you, to allow spirit to join with you, unless a teacher or assistant is present for the first few times. Remember, you only want the highest vibrational beings to join with you. If you feel apprehensive or uncomfortable with someone trying to join with you, stop it immediately! Now to get on with a couple of interesting stories.

The first time that spirit joined with me without a protective assistant, was in December 1990. I was staying with some friends in the Los Angeles area. My girlfriend Cindy had asked that I "read" her friend Sylvia. Sylvia, unable to take the day off asked us to come down to her office copy shop. It was lunch time and pretty quiet so Sylvia put a "Closed" sign on her front door for the duration of the reading.

Once there and comfortable, I dropped down immediately and gave her a very complete reading. I remember the information flowed ever so easily. During the course of things Cindy handed Sylvia a note which, in turn, she read to me. It read: "Ask about George."

Within seconds after George's name was mentioned I saw a large individual who had died of a heart condition about a month earlier. I found him to be a man who was not particularly active. Prior to his transition he was content to sit in a large chair in his apartment and now that he was in spirit he seemed equally content to sit in "his chair" under a palm tree. Among his requests was that he wanted Sylvia to check on his small brown dog. Sylvia revealed that he did indeed have a dog that fit that description. Then he said something that made no sense to me at the time. He wanted Sylvia to eat a peppermint so that he could remember what it tasted like. Later, after we had lunch together, the waitress placed a small dish containing peppermint candy canes on the table. In theory, this means that George not only knew we would be having lunch together, he must have known about the mints!

Meanwhile, as the reading continued, I started to feel George moving in on me. I felt as though I was wearing a pressure suit; lots of energy was surging through me. I asked Cindy and Sylvia to slowly lower their hands down on my arm from about a one-foot above my arm. They both stated they could "feel" a thickness, but they could not see anything.

I felt the man say "amour," to Sylvia. I could feel his overwhelming desire to hug her. Sylvia later told me that he was big bear of a man and because she is so small, he loved to wrap his arms all around her and hug her.

While all of this was going on, Cindy, who was seated directly across from me, was furiously transcribing notes. Since I was largely oblivious to what was happening, being able to later refer to these notes has been a great help in reconstructing the incident for this chapter. Cindy's notes showed that it was at this point that the transfiguration happened.

Cindy and Sylvia saw me growing in size and then she sensed an overlay of a man's face over mine. A "darkness" began to appear on the lower side of my face and then my voice started to falter, then lower in pitch, taking on the appearance of a man's voice. Cindy was becoming concerned because she could sense my obvious discomfort. She wrote down my words at the time: "Wait a minute, I think he's here; he's all around me! What made the transfiguration so apparent was the fact that George was a fairly dark-skinned Latino with the potential for a good heavy beard. My complexion is medium to fair, hence the contrast in our respective appearances was quite obvious.

Transfiguration, although not very common, is a technique whereby one dimensional level can penetrate another. The point of transition between the two levels appears to require a kind of temporary melding, a kind of molecular rearrangement achieved through the disbursement and momentary reassembling of energy patterns in the different dimension. As the medium, I must be able to function in both dimensions simultaneously for this transference of energy to occur.

I once asked spirit, "What do we, as mediums, look like from your side?" Spirit replied, "You're very interesting. We see you as an interruption of the energy of the space which you occupy." That made me think that whatever I am doing to break up the dimensions, spirit appears to be attracted, because they can, through my mediumship, participate in this molecular disbursement. In George's case, this disbursement allowed him to transfigure over me, largely, I believe for purposes of recognition and to let Sylvia know that he still cared for her very much.

Part of my concern during this particular transfiguration was that I did not have a qualified assistant to help me out of my trance state. I was still new to this stage of mediumship. I did not know what to do if George took over completely. As it turned out, it was a partial transfiguration. Only a partial transfiguration took place because although George was able to superimpose himself over me, enough of my consciousness remained within my body to prevent a full-trance situation. In retrospect, an assistant would have controlled the degree of my trance if I had gone too deeply. The assistant would have brought me out of the trance or transfiguration with the proper suggestion. As it was, Cindy did the best she could by helping me up. She walked around with me until my consciousness cleared. Then we went to lunch and I felt much better.

A client asked if it were possible for someone to "get stuck" on the other side. No, I do not believe so, anymore than a transfigured or materialized spirit could "get stuck" on this side. I know of no historical evidence to support this possibility. Emanuel Swedenborg, Andrew Jackson Davis and Rudolf Steiner — to cite three well-known, highly intuitive individuals — spent hours on the other side and yet managed to retain their physical identity and personality. What my mediumship is teaching me and what I want to share with you is an understanding of the function of energy patterns and the relative juxtaposition of the dimensions. I have learned much, and for this I am profoundly grateful and frequently amazed.

Arthur Ford and Eileen Garrett were excellent trance mediums. There are many trance mediums still living today that you can read about. Depending on the degree of their particular sensitivity and the depth of their trance, these trance mediums often reported complete removal of the conscious ego, while an entity conversed and controlled their bodies.

Today, I rarely allow a complete transfiguration to happen. I find that only a partial transfiguration or trance is necessary. Here is an example of what I mean:

About a year ago I had a friend and her husband come for an evening visit. As you know, often spirit has manipulated us for desired communication. The husband, Larry, evidentially had been thinking of his deceased mother. His mother wanted to calm his mind and tell him that she was all right. Larry's mother came forward during the course of some general conversation, and asked that I tell Larry that she was present. It was unusual because she presented herself as a much younger and beautiful woman than when she passed later in life. She came around the back side of me and put her body half way through me. She was pleasant and gentle. I saw, superimposed over my arm, the beauty of soft porcelain skin, long and jeweled fingers! Rarely do I have the privilege of seeing a transfiguration over my own body!

# XIV

## ON BECOMING A MINISTER

Initially it was not my idea to become a minister. While I was still working for a public utility, spirit spoke to me one day. Quite emphatically, spirit said that they wanted me to become a minister within a specified one-and-one half year time frame. It is confusing for me to think that if we have free will, why was I given "orders?" I was working full time for the utility company in the Auburn area, and felt that I would probably stay until I was eligible for retirement benefits. Then I would go into psychic work full time. I was getting to the point where I wanted to spend less time in this psychic world, because I was getting tired working full time and spending a great deal of time studying and practicing the psychic arts.

On one hand I wanted to quit or cut way back on my psychic work and go back to a "normal" life. I was starting to feel an invasion of my privacy, and my body and my mind were getting tired. It was just too much all at once. I felt that as a physical being I had total free choice. The choice would be mine.

Driving home (there I am again being talked to in my car!) I was telling spirit that I just about had my fill of all the work. I needed time for my privacy. Spirit then told me that if I did not wish to do this work *"the unit could be discontinued!"* *"Remember your prayer!"* I now believe that before my life began, I made a commitment to work in this field when the timing was right. At the soul level, the human, Nancy, was always destined to be a teacher. The vehicle chosen for this particular lifetime has a natural ability to teach, an ability to encourage and develop others in conscious awareness of the psychic gifts. These people would then teach others.

I knew if I would become a minister, then it had to be

within a spiritualist denomination. After researching and investigating several options, I was introduced to the Rev. Judy Fisher of the Sedona Church of the Living God. This is a Christ centered spiritualist denomination, based in Arizona. Judy and I had long discussions and considerable correspondence relative to my background and my studies. Gracefully, she accepted me as a ministerial candidate. Eventually I became a minister in her denomination. Moreover, even though I did not consciously figure the time it would take to complete her course of study, I was ordained exactly a year and a half later. The time frame was exactly as my guides had stipulated! I was ordained in the Sedona Church of the Living God on February 21, 1992. The ceremony took place in Palm Springs, California, only one month before I put in my final notice at my place of work. Spirit must have known all along, when I'd want to leave!

Has being a minister changed my life? I don't think the full implications have been revealed to me as yet. Certainly being a Christian minister has assuaged the concerns of a few of my clients. However, I have found that most people have but one concern. Clients are concerned about the quality of my reading and accuracy of the information that I and my spirit friends provide.

As a result of my ordination, I have performed a number of marriage ceremonies, a delightful chore which gives me a great deal of satisfaction. Here is a story to illustrate my delight.

It was the first Saturday in March of 1992 and I was contributing my services to the Creative Awareness Center here in Sacramento. A number of interesting people approached me for individual readings. One of these was Jackie. We discussed a number of issues and then I told her she would soon meet a man and fall in love. This individual would be a pilot. I think she was astounded by the directness of the information I gave her. Three weeks later she and Gary met and six months after that, on

September 5th, 1992, I had the privilege of uniting the two of them in marriage, during a lovely backyard ceremony here in Sacramento. They left for their honeymoon the following day in his private plane bound for Alaska.

# XV

## GOD

I believe that the power which we call God is everywhere and everything. I had a talk with spirit one day and asked him: "Where is God?" It shrugged its shoulders, raised hands and replied: "Everywhere!" as if to say incredulously, "don't you know and understand that?"

Then I asked, "where is the Jesus person?"

"So vibrationally high I cannot see Him, but He can see all."

After that I came to a more solid understanding that God is a force of energy that exists everywhere and in everything. The God force acts as a fiber that holds us together, creating a tight energy bond. The "tightness" of this energy is a reflection of how we feel on a physical, mental and an emotional level. As an intuitive I have learned to pull in this God energy from a broad spectrum of sources. This energy gives me the "power" to read on the level that I do. People can feel this energy as heat when they sit next to me, particularly if I radiate it towards them. When I travel by telephone for my readings, across town or across the country, my clients tell me they can feel this energy in the room around them.

Is that which is an atom, created by God, an ever lasting unit of energy? Everything on our small planet was here at the time of creation and is still here but in many new forms. Matter changes to energy. Energy can change to matter or another kind of energy. The cycle is always continuing.

So, curious Nancy then asks, how is it that spirit continues and survives without food? Spirit then said, "The force that holds all atoms together is pure energy, of which God and we were created. We were created by that

God force and need no substance for continuance." So maybe the atom which is held together by that God force was created to be physical matter! Oh, so easy! Oh, so confusing!

Well - just one more question then for spirit: If God and you are created with the same substance, what does vibration level mean? With more patience then I'll ever imagine this spirit said that he had given me information on a level of which I could understand. He told me I was interpreting information from him on a vibration level and then interpreting this vibration into language, similar to music. He went on to tell me that everything has a vibrational level or sound level. Everything is composed of different molecules vibrating at different levels. Even pure energy vibrates at an incredibly high rate, the higher the rate the closer to the God center. The reason for spiritual growth is to obtain the highest vibrational rate so we can join again with the original God force.

Is my interpretation of vibrational levels correct? Is it as easy to understand levels of spiritual vibrations as it is to look at a rainbow, and see that the denser the vibration, the deeper the color? The rainbow's higher vibration fades to white. Those of us that see the angelical forces notice that the higher the realm of spirits/angels, the lighter their energy fields. When I actually see the four foot by three and a half foot sphere, the color is a light milky color. Am I to understand that the vibration level is so slow as to show a "color" to me? If a higher vibrational spirit or angel were to show themselves to me would their actual sphere of energy be blinding to me? So pure of color and so high of vibration rate would the light itself be too difficult for human eyes to look at?

I know that eventually we will be able to bring all mystics together and corroborate that we all receive the same information. I feel that information is given to us only if we are ready to understand and accept the information. I believe this information is given to us in a format that coincides with the level of our evolution. Because I have seen a future incarnation for myself, will I again be a psychic? Will I ask spirit the same questions that I asked above? And will the answers be the same?

# XVI

## REINCARNATION

Today it is estimated that one person in four, or over sixty million people in the United States accept reincarnation in some form. Interest in reincarnation is growing rapidly. For these 60 million people it simply makes sense.

Many people have asked me, if the spiritual plane is so much more desirable, why do we keep coming back to this earth again over and over? My response can be stated in two short phrases: to love and be loved (physical living) and spiritual growth. Those in spirit miss the emotions, the sense of physical touch and taste, the sense of physical loving in all forms (in contrast to spiritual love).

I heard a story that a famous medium in the 1960's, had given a lecture on the after life to a crowd of 1500 people! He was so effective in his telling of such a wonderful after life that after the lecture three people apparently committed suicide! That is not my intent to convince you to discard your physical body and hurriedly go back to the spirit. My interest is to have you look at your life with a new perspective, that what you have in this lifetime is a wonderful opportunity to enjoy the full pleasures of being in the flesh. The following stories should illustrate how spirit had missed the physical body.

During one session a woman came for a reading to inquire if her father had gotten use to being back in spirit. The woman wanted to have a conversation with him. He was a very nice man. Transition had been easy for him and he had gotten use to being back in spirit, but he really missed hugging and loving his family. Amazingly he missed his first cup of coffee in the morning! He wanted his daughter to make up his favorite cup of coffee, hold the hot steaming cup and take long slow inhales of the aroma. She promised to do that the very next morning in his kitchen where they had often shared that first cup in the morning. He said he could hardly wait for the next morning to come!

Another story which was very touching was told during a group reading at the Spirit of Grace Church. This loving story convinced a lot of people that night that spirit really exists! The woman, named Vicky, asked about her grandfather. She had been taking care of this elderly grandfather in her home until his death. He was sick and death was predictable. She came to our group that night shortly after his death, to talk to him and see if he was all right. She wanted to tell him that she missed him. Grandfather was there waiting for me to connect with him. Spirits seem to know when a gathering will occur so I can assist with conversation. He immediately let me see him with new stubble on his face, and went on to let Vicky know how much he loved and missed being with her. He also wanted me to tell her how he much he missed his tub baths. He then showed me how they would lock arms and take walks together.

After a few tears, Vicky went on to explain:

"I had always been careful to have grandfather look neat and clean. He loved his baths, and that is when I would usually shave him, except on the night before he died when I felt he was too sick to be taken out of bed. He died the next day with stubble on his face. Grandfather had trouble being steady on his feet the months before his passing, but he loved being taken outdoors. To insure that he got his exercise, we had a funny way of locking our arms together (she demonstrated) so that he could get his walk." These simple loving physical pleasures are what grandfather was missing the most. Yes, the afterlife is beautiful and we can go on to pursue advanced learning, become guides to others, or just relax and pursue our interests. But after a time, we seem to miss the simplest forms of physical living and learning.

There are so many books on the benefits of reincarnation investigation, who were you, why were you born then, what were your lessons, and how did your death occur? So many opinions, and so many truths. Through my many experiences with spirit I feel that spirit comes primarily to the physical plane to love and be loved and to experience life's lessons for spiritual growth.

Here is another story and another reason why spirit wants to *"come back"* or reincarnate.

The RE/MAX Realty Systems were holding their first annual Chili Cook-Off benefiting the Children's Miracle Network here in Sacramento. My compulsion to participate in this event was literally overwhelming. As a psychic, I am frequently expected to read for people anywhere, at any time and place. I am even expected to do this while I am delightfully distracted by the wonderful smells of chili and spices wafting over from an assortment of pots, tended by some nice people who were contributing their time and energies to a worthwhile cause. Jackie, whose story I related in the previous chapter, had invited me to participate in this Chili Cook-Off benefit. It was here at the Cook-Off that I met Susan and her son Jason, the subjects of this chapter, and the beginning characters in a future book on *Death and Transition*.

It was a busy Sunday afternoon. Susan added her name and that of her son to my sign-up sheet, and patiently waited their turn. At that appointed hour they sat down and Susan got right to the point. She felt that she had two "blocks," as she expressed it, a weight problem and an inability to trust men. Being highly intuitive herself, she concluded that the root of both of these problems was somehow embedded in a past life experience.

Immediately, I saw one of the clearest past-life pictures I have ever received. I began to tell her about her life in feudal Japan, between two and three hundred years ago. I saw a Japanese woman alone, traditionally dressed, walking down a steep path at dusk. Someone jumped out from behind a bush, hit her over the head with a stone and killed her. I then saw her body fall down and fall over the edge of the path down the mountain's edge. As I described this Japanese woman, Susan told me she had the physical sensation of a hand grabbing at the base of her throat and pulling this past-life information from her. The perpetrator appeared to be someone she loved, a close male relative, a husband or a father.

"Nancy's impression that it was a close male relative stands to reason," Susan pointed out. "I felt that in my past lives I have been male many more times than a female. In this particular lifetime I chose to be a woman, and interesting, in a culture which subjugated women tremendously. It was Nancy's view that I had allowed my male energy to come to the fore in that lifetime, having opened my mouth in ways that brought shame. My death was a matter of saving face for myself and my family."

Never having met me before, Susan was astonished at the revelations this reading brought forth. She observed: "I have always had an unbelievable fear of walking downstairs or down inclines while hiking. Moreover, I have always been petrified to be alone at dusk — in fact, my fear of the dark begins at dusk. I never really understood this, but Nancy's explanation made sense."

Significantly, for years, Susan had been convinced that she would die at age twenty-eight, about the age I believed the Japanese's woman was at her death. "The realization of my fear of the dark, an early death, and steep inclines has since left me. What is amazing is that Nancy knew none of this about me and yet it all fits."

Two other points that Susan wanted to make: "I have always had a decided aversion to anything Oriental — music, culture, art, etc. Secondly, I have been involved in two marriages where trust was a major factor, and given that a husband could have once killed me, this makes sense." Susan continues to work on these issues (lessons) and in terms of accepting her own femininity, at last report she had lost fifty + pounds!

My seeing Susan in a past life as a Japanese woman may well be a figment of my imagination. In my mind, the picture was clear and vivid, but more significantly, Susan felt it to be true. "I felt Nancy's reading gave me some really good insights." Susan later observed; "I felt as I listened to her that I was hearing the truth and I knew it to be the truth!" As a result of that and subsequent readings with me, Susan is confronting her personal issues and dealing with them in a positive, forthright manner. Her openness is also allowing her own psychic gifts to flourish.

A follow up to her story is that she is currently in a positive trusting relationship. Her aversion to anything oriental has changed. It appears she "came back" to work out the issues (lessons) created during a particular past life time.

Susan's story will be expanded in a future book on death and transition, in which I tell the story about meeting her son, Jason. I gave him a reading the same day I met Susan at the Chili Cook-Off. A couple of months later, Jason, Susan's only child, was hit and killed by a drunk driver. Two months later Susan's best friend's only child, Michael, also died due to a hanging. I was able to see the death and transition of both children. I saw who greeted Jason, as he passed over and I saw the rescue of Michael. I will tell you Jason's interesting life lessons, his two month life extension. And of Michael's interesting spiritual growth. I look forward to telling you these stories!

### *A Change in Gender*

As I told the story of Susan, I mentioned that she had been a man in more past lifetimes. She seemed to prefer the life style that a male existence would offer her. Yet, she clearly was dealing with the lessons not learned while a female in a past life and again as a female in this lifetime.

My readings for hundreds of clients convinced me that a change in gender from one life's experience to another, is not only possible but probable. It is also logical. The reason is simple. Gender change allows the individual soul broader opportunities for growth. Thus a man who mistreats his wife in one lifetime may find himself mistreated as a woman in a subsequent lifetime. By the same token, an individual who treats those around him/her with love and kindness may well expect to receive the same treatment in a subsequent lifetime. In the case of a homosexual life style, those particular lessons with that life style may be why that homosexuality was chosen. I have read for many people with all kinds of life styles, and unless they tell me they are gay, I cannot tell by reading their partner if they are of the opposite sex. Remember, I read the soul level not the physical packaging. With names like Chris, Rene', Bobby, all I care about is whether the relationship is working or not, and how the relationship can be improved upon.

In 1983, I was regressed to a past life for the first time. I had many doubts about the process, indeed about the whole idea of past lives. But a friend said to me, "I dare you," and being the kind of person I am, I immediately jumped to the challenge.

I was regressed way back, back to a lifetime in Egypt. I was a young man taking care of my father's wheel making business and bored to death. I became a message runner between military camps. I'm a runner in this lifetime. Interesting! It was not a particularly memorable lifetime, but it did show me how far I have progressed since then.

More recently I have seen myself in a past lifetime as a very old African-American man in the South. I determined the locale by the terrain. I died peacefully in my rocking chair on the porch, an impression etched vividly in my memory. The time of my passing was either spring or fall; the date being '22 — 1922? The twentieth century suggests itself, as a colleague, Camille, has had a similar past life memory and she and I both suspect we were friends then, as we are now. She drew a picture of herself as well as her memory could recall past life flashbacks. I distinctly remember that in that southern lifetime that I was very psychic and served as a counselor for folks throughout the area. I was also a very large man, huge, in fact, and probably served as a protector of others during my younger days. The same gift that individual had and used during that lifetime, I have and use today.

I also recall a life during World War II. I feel I was a female, blue eyed, blond hair. Apparently I changed gender again for this short life in the early 1940's. I have the feeling that I am in Europe. I feel five years old, and remember something going into my eyes and killing me instantly.

Finally, there is the question, why don't I remember my past lives? I believe the present "ego" is not the "ego" of past vehicles. I feel the current "ego" is a combination of past ego traits and a combination of traits specific to your environment and family. Were it possible for us to "physically" return to an earlier lifetime, I doubt we would recognize ourselves. At least superficially, that earlier individual would appear to be a complete stranger.

Shouldn't each incarnation present new latitude and new freedoms? Should grudges and recriminations from a previous existence affect the learning opportunities afforded in a new lifetime?

As we pass through many lands and many civilizations, each of us adds new experiences to the totality of our ego. We must value and savor each fresh opportunity. It becomes self-defeating not to do so. At the same time I am the first to recognize that certain past life information, whether it comes directly through a sensitive like myself or through hypnotic regression, may prove extraordinarily beneficial in dealing with and perhaps rectifying if not solving certain problems in this life. A good example of this process was shown in Susan's story.

Ultimately, however, the focus of each new life must be on this life if we are to maximize the learning provided through each individual life experience. My advice is to **learn, grow,** and **enjoy.**

# XVII

## KARMA

Karma, of course, goes hand-in-hand with reincarnation. As a definition I might suggest:
> The total impact of a person's actions and conduct during the successive phases or lives of her or his development, ultimately determining the individual's destiny.

To sum up the concept of karma as "an eye for an eye, a tooth for a tooth," places a purely negative connotation on this idea of karma. Karma is far more encompassing and essentially means there is a balance in the universe.

Karma can work for us in many ways, individually and collectively. I was doing a telephone reading for a woman in a Pacific Northwest community one evening and she said "Every time I turn around I meet someone I think I know; I look into their eyes and I am pulled into them."

As she talked I saw her entire community, a valley in the center; mountains on the sides. There appeared to be a group reincarnation in process. My vision may have been of the community where they were in a past life because of what I "heard" clairaudiently. I heard the words that this city is a "karmically controlled arena," meaning that many of the people in the community were collectively coming back at a specific time to deal with certain issues together. The television program "Sightings" mentioned Lake Elsinore, in Southern California as being a similar community where many of its residents appeared to have a collective, karmic, past-life relationship.

Group disasters such as plane crashes can facilitate group karma. Large numbers of people make their transitions together in order that they might make a group return to their next life. Karma can thus include making a predetermined transition in order to be properly "positioned" for the successive lifetime. For reasons pointed out in the previous chapter, we rarely have conscious memory of a previous lifetime. However, I do believe that each time we "recycle" we bring with us characteristics of past lifetimes. The soul level subliminally retains a consciousness of each of those lifetimes.

In addition to working out past karma in this lifetime, I believe that we can create karma in this lifetime and then need to work it out at a later time. How many of you know people without money who obtain inheritances, win the lottery and then just to fiddle it away, or lose it foolishly? Perhaps these winners had an opportunity to learn a lesson, but for whatever reason their reward was taken away. How about couples who marry, have children and then divorce? The parent that had trouble with the children marries again only to acquire more children. Maybe the lesson was not learned the first time around. Maybe the parent needed to learn how to nuture or be responsible! Oh yes, I imagine everyone reading the last couple of sentences can relate those stories to someone.

What if you don't believe in karma for this lifetime or a next? Will you gamble and live your life with no regard to outcome? You may have your lessons given right back to you. This sounds like good after dinner conversation.

### I'm My Own Grandpa

In the 1940's, Jaffe and Latham wrote an amusing song called "I'm My Own Grandpa". It was quite popular for a number of years. A man I know fits this song in a spiritual sense. The gentleman believes he is his own great-grandfather. While undergoing a past-life regression through a crystal technique in Sedona, Arizona he received information confirming his belief in his spiritual lineage. The great-grandfather made his transition in the South in 1930. The soul essence that was the grandfather experienced a rebirth in the Southwest in the 1950's in the form of the present day gentleman. Is this possible and why?

Certainly it is possible that family members would still be alive so that the individual could work out negative or positive karma that was left incomplete by the great-grandfather. Or they may wish to inherent the same physical abilities that they possessed in a prior lifetime. Since this gentleman, told me of this regression, I have talked to and read for no less than eight people who have come back in a subsequent generation as their own grand children. Possibly they wished to interact with their own children both as parent and child!

# XVIII

## SOULMATES

Not infrequently an individual will come to me for a reading and ask: "Where is the man or woman whom I'm going to love for the rest of my life - my **soulmate**?"

In a previous chapter, I touched briefly on soulmates and how the phenomena of soul mates could relate to soul vibration compatibility. The soul (mate) essence can and does appear, but not necessarily in this lifetime as a lover. There may be souls whom we cherish more than others. However this cherished soul may be a teacher that you especially trust, or a parent or a best friend. To always be lovers in each subsequent lifetime, how could we grow and learn our lessons if the soul level essence would involve the same pairing in each lifetime! Perhaps you have been lovers or companions to hundreds of people in as many lifetimes. You care for these people on a soul level and perhaps have exercised the option to help one or more of them in each lifetime. As we open up ourselves to serve in this capacity, we are nourishing a very real part of our soul's purpose.

You'll have a sense of importance about these relationships where individuals come into your life for a purpose. I'll call these people "markers." As one individual may be a marker for you, equally so are you a marker for one, dozens, or hundreds of others. These markers tend to have a profound effect on each of us although we may not be aware of the significance of the impact. Reflect back for a moment and remember those people you have especially cared about. Consider the importance they have had in your life. A number of those individual markers should come to mind.

I know that many of you want me to affirm that soulmates in the role of lovers, are waiting for each of us but

I've only come across one couple in doing this work whom I felt were soulmates. They too, believed they were soulmates. I met them at the RE/MAX Realty Systems Chili Cook-Off benefit I mentioned in an earlier chapter. As their reader, you can well imagine, it was a delightful experience being exposed to their feelings for one another. The woman, a nurse, came over for a reading. As she sat down I felt her soul but there was yet another soul partially superimposed over hers. Astonished, I asked her about her current love interest as I assumed a deep soul connection.

"Yes," she replied, "this is my second marriage and I am so in love and it is wonderful."

After we finished the reading she left. Later in the day a man came over to me for a reading. He sat down and I said: "Wow, you're the second person today who has..." and he cut me off with a smile. "You know, that was my wife with whom you spoke earlier today."

I was so amazed. Clearly, there exists within us, the ability for such closeness, souls passing together through eternity, each soul learning the lessons it needs separately in contact with others. Finally, when the timing is right, an intermesh occurs such as I found that afternoon. As desirous as this union may be and as frustrating as the waiting process may seen, we must remember that if contact with our soulmate were to come too soon in the evolutionary process of our soul's existence, we might well miss the benefit of interacting with others. Souls can connect and travel through history together and if they touch as lovers, there clearly is a special kind of magic.

Another woman came to me and asked: "Was my son a lover in a past lifetime? Although we don't have that kind of relationship now, I feel such a connection."

I told her without equivocation, "you've had at *least* three lifetimes together, all the way from the beginning of time." But were they soulmates? Not necessarily. Perhaps these two souls were just very significant and reoccurring markers for each other through the course of time.

If you don't find that perfect person this time around, there is undoubtedly a reason. Relax and go with the flow. Your learning process will be so much more meaningful. I believe that the soul is pure energy and pure mental thought and yet with an enduring consciousness that transcends time. It is all part of God's manifold blessing for each and every one of us.

# XIX

## DISCOVERING A PURPOSE IN LIFE

During the course of one of my lectures, a gentleman in his late thirties asked me: "Just what am I supposed to do in this lifetime?"

I looked at him and then said to the audience: "This man has had the most spiritual growth in the shortest amount of time I have ever felt in anyone. He is what I call a natural healer and a teacher, a man filled with a great deal of learned compassion.

"This man never knew what life was in the past," I continued, "and his karma in this lifetime is not to deny his right to life. There was a time in the past when he was not a particularly nice individual. He ended many lives through the use of a sharp instrument; now he is carrying the scars of others." Then, looking at him directly, I asked: "Have you ever noticed how much you sometimes hurt in the area just above your stomach, and the pain made no sense?"

"Yes," he nodded in agreement.

"Well, guess where you used to stab people? In this lifetime," I explained, "you are learning how to deal with people on an entirely different level, which is why life hasn't been so good to you. Of all of the people in this room, you have really had a good many hard knocks in this life. That's because you had to learn your humility first. When you start teaching, the pain in your stomach will cease."

I quoted a poem in the first chapter on the purpose of life. That poem states that if we cannot love our life, how can a path be shown to us, that will allow a life purpose to develop. How many of us are involved only in the mundane, living only from moment to moment? Yes, times can be hard, but some of the most spiritual people I know are the ones who have allowed themselves time to seek spiritual growth in the face of adversity. We must allow lessons to be presented to us and to learn from these lessons.

Some people will come to me and say they want to run away from the life they have now. They want to quit their present money path and search for the passion/purpose path. I have often said that I wish that I could have started helping people twenty years ago. For as many people that I have counseled how many more could I have helped with problems like this. My psychic path wasn't shown to me earlier in life because I just was not ready. I had to experience my life's lessons. If at twenty-five, I had started with this psychic gift, would I have understood the problems people brought to me? Would I have had the compassion to want to help them?

I believe all events of destiny that lead to the discovery of our purpose in life, will be presented at the correct time. You are searching now, even as you read this book, and that should tell you that you are getting closer to the discovery of your true purpose in this life. Please don't overlook what you have already accomplished in this life whether it was important or whether it was trivial. One or two events that appear trivial could have been your purpose in this life or could have set you on your life's path. And perhaps from this day forth, you will be allowed to develop and expand your spiritual life and psychic gifts.

By meditation and getting in touch with our spiritual guides we can escalate our spiritual growth and be presented with our purpose. Have you said a "high risk prayer?" By getting in touch with your guides, or saying that all important pledge, you will notice doors being opened up to you. And as you seek your path, with love and understanding help others also in their search, for that may be your purpose in this life. I believe it is my purpose.

# XX

## EARTH CHANGES

Living in California, I am constantly asked to predict climate changes, and above all, earthquakes, including "the big one!" Being on the Pacific Rim, "the ring of fire," as it is sometimes called, earthquakes are something Californians have come to expect. I am very sensitive to the movement of the earth's crust and the slippage of the tectonic plates which create earthquakes. I am also sensitive to the magnetic pull of the core of the earth. As the pressure builds up between plate surfaces, I feel a tension and a pressure around my body like a change in the barometer. If you also feel this, the best way to develop this psychic trigger is to keep a diary of feelings. This diary will confirm your feelings and help you ascertain the correctness of your predictions. As you acknowledge one psychic gift, other gifts will also open up.

I usually won't go out of my way for sensational purposes, predicting earthquakes, or other natural disasters. I don't feel that is what my guides have directed me to do. I personally feel it could cause undue stress or panic. I can't and do not want to be put in that position. But if asked, whether in private or public setting, a question regarding these issues, I will answer discreetly.

In anticipation of "the big one," people ask me if they should consider moving away from California. I am in no position to say (though I may get an idea of where an earthquake could come) because I don't know when "the big one" is going to happen. I suspect, however, as we get close to the event I will sense it and, as I tell my audiences with a smile on my face, "When the time comes, and spirit wants me to leave, I'll be the first one to pack. You follow me!" Incidentally, I will often overpack when going on a trip - because I can't even predict my own weather conditions!

    Individuals with my kind of sensitivity can also feel potential tidal wave activity. I recently met a lady who says that she is part of a small group that are in constant contact with the University of California Davis medical facility involved in a research group there. She prefers not to be recognized, but she tells me that she has been sensitive to earth changes ever since she was a small child. She told her doctor about her unusual sensitivity to earth and tidal phenomena and the doctor connected her with this research group in Davis.

## XXI

### "Lady Luck"

Should you develop your psychic gift for your personal gain, say at gambling? I know a few women who live in Auburn who are frequent gamblers and they win most of the time. I feel they are using what appears to be a natural instinct for those "lucky machines." Yes, that can also be called a psychic instinct, but perhaps it is also a sense of careful observation techniques and strong hunches combined. I personally do not know anyone who calls themselves psychic, who has the ability to gamble using psychic techniques whether the ability is used to zero in on the lucky machine or the lucky card table. Now that does not preclude the use of psychic techniques by professional gamblers. I had a friend tell me that the Reno casinos hire professional *"watchers"* for those kinds of people.

A combination of several things deters me from counting on my winnings. First, the intensity of emotion due to winning would feel the same as losing. Perhaps sometimes the intense feeling of losing is greater than winning. So if I walked up to a machine, would I feel the losing vibes or winning vibes? Have you ever noticed the intense energy when walking into a casino? All those people, getting so excited or *soooo* depressed. The intensity in a casino is almost as bad as when I was cooped up in a kid packed theater trying to watch last summer's big hit at a Saturday matinee. After two hours of getting bombarded with screaming energy, I was a nervous wreck for another two hours afterward. The same principle would also apply in the casino. Its very difficult for me to push aside all that energy in order to concentrate on which machine to play.

But, my bad luck at gambling hasn't stopped me from

advising friends of a "good" or "bad" gambling effort. Back in June of 1992, during one of our Wednesday night psychic circles at the Spirit of Grace Church two sisters, Kathy and Marlene, brought their parents to the circle. Mom and Dad had their fiftieth wedding anniversary coming up in July and I thought it was interesting that I could see fireworks around them.

"Congratulations," I told them and then asked, "How do you plan to celebrate this marvelous occasion and do you have a question for me this evening?"

"I think we're going to go gambling," Mom said.

"Great," I responded, "where do you plan to go?

"Las Vegas."

At that moment I got a view of Mom walking up to a roulette table. Next to her was standing a small, dark-haired man and a taller, somewhat larger man, better built, with white hair. "When you go to Vegas it must be you are supposed to go to this table because I see so much excitement there and I feel you're going to win!"

A month later I saw them again. "How did it go; how did you do in Las Vegas? Did you win?"

"We lost. We went to Reno instead."

"Remember," I told them, "you told me you were going to Vegas and I saw you winning there."

Well, the next time they did go to Las Vegas. They found the table with the two men as I had described them, and they won. I am not certain of the amount but it was several hundred dollars.

My friend Renee provides us with another story about lady luck. I was working a psychic fair in Roseville one weekend and Renee came by, terribly depressed over a boyfriend.

"I'm upset," she said. "I'm going to take the day off and go to Reno. Should I gamble?"

Instantly I knew that she would win. It just felt so

good. "You're going to win," I told her, "and you're going to have a great time!"

On her return, Renee called me. "Guess what, I won!, just as you predicted."

"Well," my curiosity getting the best of me I asked, "how much did you win?"

"I won 2,500 nickels!"

Two thousand five hundred nickels are a lot of nickels!

Priscilla and Lorraine did much better. These two women are hair dressers and they have a very nice shop in Loomis, a comfortable suburban, rural community about forty-five minutes from Sacramento. Lorraine approached me on one occasion and told me she and Priscilla were going to Reno. "Am I going to win?" she asked.

"Yes, it feels wonderful," was my response. "I want you to go to a place that has a lot of bright lights, lots of reflection, a lot of glitter. That's the place where you'll win. Do you play the slot machines?"

"Yes, I do."

So the two women headed east to Reno. They parked their car and began walking around Reno's principle gambling area. Lorraine remembered my suggestion about the lights and the glitter and they decided to try a casino that also had a psychic fair going on. As Lorraine looked up she noticed lots of tinsel hanging from the ceiling, so much so "I was almost blinded," she said. "I knew this had to be the place." Coming out several hundred dollars ahead for her efforts, it was a good afternoon for Lorraine!

# XXII

## *OTHER LIFE FORMS*

My intuitive ability functions on a number of different levels. I am constantly surprised as new possibilities open up for me. I find I can now see other life forms. I can see those life forms which represent other dimensions; what I call "alternate energy beings." When true channeling occurs, as opposed to mediumship, I find the source of the channeling may be functioning in a different dimension from our own dimension. The channel must transcend his or her own vibration to be able to receive information in this different dimension.

When I see individuals who can channel in this format, I have the feeling of very great distance. I see this distance as a "tunnel of energy" and I can feel "the source" or alternate energy being at the end of the tunnel of energy. I then feel the alternate energy being's mass, but I can't always see them. The power of the energy source invariably hits me on the right side of my forehead. In psychism or mediumship the impression is made to the side of my head above my ear and towards the back of the brain. Receiving this power is achieved by an **"overlapping"** or a **"folding"** of time and space and thus, in effect, there is no distance between the source and the channel, no distance between alternate energy being and me.

A woman named Lydia came for a reading. "Read my guides. They're not paying attention to me!" she said. "I want to know what's going on with them. I am having some problems and I want you to ask them to figure it out for me."

I saw these guides. Three of them. The one in the center was a woman whom I recognized as being very significant in the early days of the Theosophical movement in

England and in this country. The woman said "there's someone else that wants to speak to her." She then stepped aside, revealing a tunnel surging with energy. For two hours I was out-of-control (in a positive manner), dealing with aspects of evolution and drawing constellations — information which was far beyond my own understanding. This information was coming from a very high evolved "living" being from another dimension. This was one of the first times I "channeled." What was interesting is that spirit was working with him! In addition, Lydia was unaware that one of her four guides was a living being, she assumed all her guides to be spirits.

Lydia did access her guides, but not until they enjoyed the medium they were working through first! Her guides said that our mentality is like the first day of pre-school compared to graduate studies. They sometimes have a difficult time translating universal matters into a very basic level of understanding, but that since we are very eager for information it makes it a pleasure to guide us.

I am also beginning to touch into the world of elementals. Many individuals, such as Geoffrey Hodson, *Fairies at Work and at Play*, claim to be able to observe this world of fairies, brownies, elves, gnomes, sylphs, mannikins, undines and sea spirits, devas and a whole panoply of nature spirits. I have yet to acquire this ability with any degree of facility. I certainly see spirit with much more clarity than I did four years ago when I took my first tentative steps into psychism and mediumship. Are elementals next? Stay tuned.

# XXIII

## CONCLUSION

For many years I really didn't know who I was, what I was doing or where I was going. I could never really measure my life because I never knew how I felt about myself. All that changed four years ago.

In these pages I have tried to demonstrate something of what I have learned, the growth I have experienced, and the contrast between the two worlds in which I walk. Clearly I enjoy doing what I do. I enjoy teaching the psychic arts to others. I am always amazed at the humor of spirit and the fun I have practicing this gift particularly with groups of people.

In the section to follow are guidelines I have set up to help you develop your psychic abilities. Jim, who went into spirit in February of this year told me of a friend whose father was a Spiritualist Minister. This friend waited until he was in his mid-fifties before he decided to become a minister as his father had been. That man practiced every day for twelve years before he came out of the dark! He never gave up. The man is now in his seventies and is a minister in the National Association. He lives outside of Reno, Nevada. So the moral of that story is to never give up or get discouraged. I remember how frustrated I was that this psychic gift did not blossom until my early forties however just like the 70 year old man from Nevada, I just wasn't ready!

Finally, this gift has allowed me to specifically deal with the needs and concerns of hundreds of individuals from all walks of life and from many places throughout the globe. Gratefully, today I am blessed with my **Life, Love** and **Laughter,** and a very special **Path, Purpose** and a **Passion** which I am privileged to share every day of my life. To my clients, friends and those of you meeting me for the first time through the pages of this book, thank you for walking down this unfolding path with me and for allowing me to share my thoughts and experiences with you. Isn't it wonderful to be on this exciting spiritual journey together?

In an earlier chapter, I told of a young woman facing an unusual situation regarding an unexpected pregnancy. I promised that by the time the book came to press, we will have found out the decision she faced and the choices she made.

This young woman decided to continue with the pregnancy. She had the child, but the sex was not as predicted, it was a male child. What was interesting, she had consulted with two other psychics after deciding to keep the pregnancy and they also said it would be a female. The child evidently is a sensitive gentle male. Even with that the child has the features and coloring as I had predicted. Also, the child's father does not want to participate in the upbringing. The man she was interested in, did transfer to her unit. But at the moment he is still married and she is honoring his relationship with his wife and has not interfered in his relationship. Another interesting fact, he had been trained by her to cover her responsibilities while she was on maternity leave.

Please watch for my next book — *Two Worlds — Ghosts, Goblins and Spirits* — to come out next year. Future books in the *Two World* Series are: *Death and Transition — A Personal Experience, Time and Harmony,* and *Reincarnation, Which Lifetime Affects You Now.*

## HOW TO CHAPTER - MEDITATION AND BASIC PSYCHIC DEVELOPMENT

Before we start discussing how to become more psychic, we should address the primary basics of anyone seriously contemplating working in the psychic realm. I'm not addressing those individuals who use a tool exclusively. Anyone wanting to use their inherent psychic ability should first learn how to meditate. Meditation is the first step in learning how to focus, to concentrate on an item or person to receive information.

People who sit with me, or have watched me address a large group, watch me momentarily relax. I have condensed the steps, that I will list below, into perhaps 45 to 60 seconds. I sometimes laugh and say, "I'm the world's fastest meditator!" Getting ready to read for any length of time, from one client to an entire day of fair activity, I will normally meditate just once. Remember in previous chapters, the idea is to meditate to a level where you'll be able to use a specific psychic ability at will and be able to receive information.

There are many meditation books available on the market, from how to develop your ability to accessing your angel or spirit guides. The primary steps, are to ground yourself, relax, remove clutter from your mind, learn who you are, and then be a receiver.

Find a location, where you can safely spend an allocated amount of time every day. Make sure that you will not be interrupted. Make yourself comfortable, sitting on the floor or in a chair. I do not recommend the bed. You don't want to fall asleep!

At this point, I will focus on my intent, to be God focused, saying a prayer to put my inner being at peace. Whatever your spiritual point of view allow the God force to protect and guide the session you are about to enter.

While sitting, with lights dimmed, with or without

relaxing background music, start relaxing your body from the top of your head all the way to your toes. If you want, or feel you need extra help relaxing, use a visualization tool. Some people like to visualize a glowing ball of golden light entering their forehead and pushing the stress of the day and mind chatter all through their body into the core and healing force of mother earth. I like sitting and I gently shake all the muscle groups starting from my head to my feet until I feel heavy and solid against the chair I am sitting. An observer would not detect the shaking.

At this point you should be listening to your heart beating, the blood rushing through your veins and pulsing in your neck. I am now at a point where I feel I can identify all the parts of "Nancy". Knowing who **you** are and knowing all **your** borders is very important to know when channeled or psychic information comes to you. Knowing yourself gives you one of the most important tools that can help you know that the information you receive is *not* from you or your imagination but is from spirit.

Now the next step is very important. You'll need to practice meditating, relaxing your entire human vehicle and allow the psychic part of you to emerge. Pay attention to how you feel at that particular moment. The most basic way I can describe that feeling, is, as through my electrical energy field around me grows denser and then spreads out into the room. People sitting near me when I meditate down to this level can feel it about ten to fifteen feet from me.

Each psychic gift I access has a particular body/mind feeling. Often in groups people will hear me say that there are so many psychic abilities we can access that I call them 31 flavors. I can "turn on" two or three psychic switches at a time. When addressing a group, I can bounce between people and read the aura of one and the past life of another or emotional feelings of a companion of yet someone else within seconds of each. To do that, I had to identify what each switch feels like to access requested information from a client. Beginning psychics sometimes limit themselves to one type of ability until they are comfortable with the feeling. They then go on adding to their abilities as they learn each body/mind feeling and psychic "switch."

Now you are probably saying, "how is this done?" Without sounding too repetitive, practice, practice, practice. Practice meditating to a level to turn on a particular psychic gift and then attempt reading an object or person.

Just starting out, you may not know what information you'll receive when attempting to read for the first few times. As the information comes to you pay attention to how you feel. Remember that psychic "flavor, that body/mind feeling" and after a few times you'll go directly to that "flavor" without hesitation after relaxing. Practice reading objects of anyone who gives you permission or if someone asks you to read. I personally feel reading someone without their permission and then relaying that information to them is an invasion of privacy.

If you are serious about developing your psychic ability, the above steps should be an exercise you look forward to doing daily. Determine what your driving force is. What is your goal? Are you developing your own intuitive gifts for yourself, or to assist others? How much time will you spend each day? How much time you will want to spend is important to your growth. The amount of time spent and effort put into practicing your talent will determine how quickly you grow.

My first six weeks of psychic development, I worked only one day a week performing readings at the Spirit of Grace Church. However I scheduled daily practice of meditation. After those initial six weeks, I had my first private session. In a month I had at least one client a day in addition to the weekly group sessions at the church. One year and eleven months later I walked away from my

24 year career to work at this full time, feeling nervous but confident that I would have a successful career in the psychic arts. If your goal is to use your gifts for full time employment, please understand that a person's particular growth is determined by their inherent supersensitive nervous system. We all progress at different rates. Please don't get frustrated or jealous if others seem to progress faster. Everything is in divine order. Those who progress faster may be directed by the unseens to hurry because of an immediate purpose. The developing psychic may not even be aware of this unseen help.

Again, the steps necessary to develop your psychic ability are to:

- Find a safe, quiet haven accessible daily or weekly - uninterrupted.
- Determine a comfortable sitting spot.
- Dim lights or darken room to a twilight environment.
- Select a soothing background music if you desire.
- At this point, say your particular prayer of protection.
- Use a visualization tool, or focus on each body part. Relax each part of your body.
- In a relaxed state, feel your body and become familiar with your person.
- Bring about the feeling of complete relaxation.
- Feel your energy field become denser, and move into the room.

> *As you practice reading objects or people, this meditation activity will become easier each time you do it.*

- Practice moving your energy into the room and then back again, gain control.

*As you become more proficient, you'll gain control over unwarranted random reading of people thus gaining control of your life. You will also become more proficient at ignoring distractions such as unexpected noises.*

Practice your new meditation and relaxation techniques in other areas of your life. The quiet atmosphere of your meditation sanctuary is excellent for beginners. But if you wish to use your gift publicly, you'll need to bring yourself to a psychic awareness level while in front of not only a potential client, but perhaps a group. Don't publicly announce to those at work or while in an elevator that "you are dropping down - so don't bother me." Your associates will think you are a sandwich short of a full picnic. Pick a moment, when you naturally would have an opportunity to quiet yourself, or collect yourself from a stressful situation. After sitting and relaxing through the above steps, you may be surprised to find yourself collected and ready to go again with renewed energy.

Relax and enjoy the unlimited joy in learning your true nature and your greatest potential as a psychic spiritual human being.

# BOOK GIFT CERTIFICATES

**Treat your friend/family member to a book!**

Book gift certificates offer a special 20% discount from the suggested retail price.

Catalogs will gladly be sent upon request. Book orders must be prepaid. Include shipping and handling (US postal book rate).

**Send orders to:**

Nancy Matz
Creative Solutions
866-602-8966
www.NancyMatz.com

\_\_\_\_ **YES!** Enter my name on your Mailing List, and _____ send me your free catalog.

Name: _____ Signature: _____

Address: _____

City: _____ State/Province _____ Zip _____

Country: _____ Home Phone: ( ) _____

**Total**

Qty. _____ at $11.00 ea.      $ _____

Please add S&H **$2.50 first book**      $ _____

and **$.50 each additional book.**      $ _____

California residents add 8.25% tax.      $ _____

**Total Enclosed (US Funds Please)** $ _____

Make checks payable to CREATIVE SOLUTIONS